VW Camper –
Inspirational Interiors
Bespoke and Custom Interior Designs

VW Camper –
Inspirational Interiors

Bespoke and Custom Interior Designs

David Eccles

The Crowood Press

First published in 2008 by
The Crowood Press Ltd
Ramsbury, Marlborough
Wiltshire SN8 2HR

www.crowood.com

This impression 2013

British Library Cataloguing-in-Publication Data
A catalogue record for this book is available from the British Library.

ISBN 978 1 84797 070 1

Disclaimer
Some words, model names and designations are trademarked and are the property of the
trademark holder. They have been used for identification purposes only and this is not an official
publication.

   Whilst every effort has been made to ensure the accuracy of all material, the author and
publisher cannot accept liability for loss resulting from error, mis-statement, inaccuracy or
omission contained herein. The author welcomes any corrections or additional information.

Photography by David Eccles.

Additional photographs courtesy: Darren Larwood and Pooch, Phil Osborne and Mike Johnson,
Simon Coldwell; Andrew Spencer; Will McLaughlin; Dave Sutherland; Ant Edensor; Andy Holder;
John Thompson; Julian Hunt; David Bond; Alan Cutts; Alex Fenton; Mike Wood; Craig Robinson;
Viv John and Mike Moore; Simon Fitzjohn, Geoff Parker; Stef Leonard; Brendan O'Farrell; Phil
Taylor; Richard Newton; David Bunce; Pete Boxall; Tom Steele; Jo Farrington.

Acknowledgements
Thanks to all those owners who willingly talked to me about their campers and kindly let me
photograph them. Thanks also to Jon at Calypso Campers, Simon at Interior Motive, Vaughn and
Tim at Custom Classic and Retro for taking time to help and for suggesting interiors to include,
and to all the businesses listed in the Gazetteer.

Dedication
This book is dedicated to my wife Cee, who sometimes felt like a VW widow during the year I
spent writing it, but who was always there with advice and support.

Photograph previous page: 1964 Split Screen Camper (*see* Chapter 2). Photograph courtesy of
Andrew Spencer.

Typeset and designed by D & N Publishing
Lambourn Woodlands, Hungerford, Berkshire.

Printed and bound in India by Replika Press Pvt. Ltd.

contents

ABOVE: Five generations of the VW Bus have been produced since production started in 1950.
RIGHT: Bespoke interiors often mix traditional layouts with modern materials, colours and designs.

The VW Camper was the first motor caravan to be available to a large market, and it has become a classic icon, conjuring up nostalgia and rich in romantic associations of freedom, individuality and optimism. Increasing affluence during the fifties, and the emergence of an affordable, versatile and reliable vehicle that could serve a variety of purposes, meant that motor caravanning, once the province of the well-off upper middle classes, was now within the reach of many families. Right from 1951, the new VW Transporter's possibilities as a campervan were obvious, and during 1951–52 Westfalia produced a few hand-built, fully kitted-out versions.

However, they saw that a bigger market could be tapped into by producing something that would be multi-functional, and in 1953 the Westfalia Camping Box was born. This was a lift-in, lift-out camping set that would easily fit in the Kombi with its removable seats, and consisted of a fold-out bed, seating, a table and a cooker. At around the same time, Dormobile began fitting special folding seats, cookers and elevating roofs to vehicles, though as import duties were high, they used UK marques such as Austin and Landrover for their conversions. By the mid-fifties, such was the demand that Westfalia had introduced a fully fitted affair, and in 1957 Peter Pitt (Canterbury Pitt) and Jack White (Devon Coachworks) introduced family campers on the VW base in the UK. Since then countless variations of camping interiors have come and gone…

Early interiors used quality wood for the cabinets and were craftsman built.

Camping equipment was simple and low tech, with basic sleeping, cooking, eating and washing facilities, an evaporation or ice-chilled coolbox, and storage for clothes and bedding. Though each converter took, and continues to take, a slightly different route regarding how to lay out or incorporate camping facilities, what to include as basic or optional, and interior finish and trim, they all work from the idea that the interior has to be designed for use as a living room, kitchen, dining room and bedroom, depending on how things are rearranged. Whilst some conversions offered full-on, self-contained

Early 1960s Devon interior, updated with new curtains and seat covers, showing the classic dinette seating arrangement.

camping interiors, others went for a multi-purpose, flexible 'weekender' approach, combining people carrier with basic sleeping and cooking facilities, using seats that could face forwards for travelling or be arranged dinette-style, and with cupboard space and pull-out beds.

The rectangular space of the VW's cargo area is ideal for designing a flexible layout, but has the restriction of a sliding side door (or two opening cargo

This 1972 Moonraker features the swing-out cooker cabinet.

doors in the case of pre-1967 models), giving three sides on which to arrange seats and cabinets, plus the area at the rear above the engine bay. Working with this restriction, converters have come up with many ingenious ways to maximize use of space, including door-mounted cookers or cabinets, cookers that swing out, meaning they can be used outside, and even a cooker sited in the cab that fits behind the passenger seat. Seats can be arranged to face forwards or backwards; tables can be mounted on the floor, sidewall or cabinets, or can even use the spare wheel as a base for outside use; sinks fold out from under seats; and sliding rear drawers are designed to be accessed via the tailgate or from inside the bus. Plus of course, every converter has ingenious ways of maximizing every inch of space for storage.

When researching the stock interiors guide (*VW Camper: The Inside Story*, The Crowood Press), the main thing to strike me was the seemingly infinite additional methods and ways that owners themselves come up with to adapt and refine traditional and tested layouts, whether by combining ideas from several different conversions, or by taking a radical,

Original interiors always attract attention at shows, as they are living history.

completely new approach to traditional layouts with circular seating or curving cabinets. These interiors take individual design routes, and it is this that is celebrated in this companion book.

One of the major attractions about the VW bus, apart from its iconic looks, associations with freedom and rugged reliability, is the way owners take the bus to heart and into their family, and set about personalizing each one through both exterior and interior design and styling. Most owners also give their bus a name! Over the years most campers have seen extensive use, and unless you are lucky enough to find a complete, original condition camper, or one that has been fully restored, then some work will inevitably need to be done to bring the interior to the standard you want.

LEFT: *The Westfalia SO 34 had distinctive plaid fabrics, and featured a flip-over front seat that makes L-shaped seating.*
RIGHT: *Arcomobil Campers had a very different table/seat layout.*

commissioning) an interior that will serve your own needs is a daunting yet exciting task, and within the following pages you will find many different sorts of interior to admire and inspire. Some have been built on a budget from scratch by the owner, some have been adapted and revamped, others are bespoke one-offs, built to the owners' designs. Some recreate period styling with a contemporary twist; others bring in completely modern designs using new materials and shapes.

What has emerged from talking to owners about their interiors is the way each design and layout has been carefully tailored to their own specific needs. The common starting point is to carefully consider what the bus is to be used for, and to draw up a list of absolutely essential items. Whilst some want the full-on, camping-in-style experience with portaloos, sinks, TVs and modern cookers, others simply want to have somewhere to sit and relax in, a kind of outdoor living room. Modern hob grills and washing facilities are essential for

Whilst an intact, period perfect, original 1960s camper has all the appeal of life when it was much simpler, they were designed in a very different time with different customer expectations. Sinks and fridges were not considered essential, cookers were often very basic, and beds required intricate laying down of boards. Changing lifestyles and advances in technology mean that things such as a decent sound system and flip-down DVD player are now becoming essential.

Old campers may have charm and appeal, but they are not always the most comfortable or practical of vehicles! Designing and building (or

ABOVE: *Canterbury Pitt campers had a unique door-mounted cooker cabinet.*
BELOW: *The T3 Jokers followed the route used by many modern conversions, including the T5 California, with all units running down one side.*

A stock Canterbury Pitt interior has had seats covered in grey leather to harmonize with the original grey interior panels.

some; others prefer to cook and wash outside in an awning, opting to maximize living space. Then there are those who set out to create something that is eye catching and cutting edge, and which pushes the boundaries of interior design. Whether spartan minimalist or decadent luxury, an interior is an owner's own personal living space and a reflection of his or her personality and lifestyle. Whatever the design approach, the key words that come up again and again are that the interior must be practical, stylish and distinctive.

Once facilities and layout are decided, the fun bit begins. Like moving into a new home, a new interior needs dressing with fabrics and accessories that also reflect the taste and personality of the owner. Whether funky and fun, smooth and subtle, retro or radical, the interior styling is as important as its practicality. Colours are carefully chosen to coordinate and harmonize, often echoing the exterior colours of the camper. The interiors depicted here all work from the basic design tenets of unity, form and functionality, whether family camper or cutting edge catching custom, they have been designed to create something suited to an owner's specific needs. Freed from the constraints of mass production or an in-house conversion style, a bus owner starting out to design his or her own interior can mix and match ideas, turning a dated look into something modern and contemporary, or creating something new, incorporating modern technology and lifestyle needs. Many of the interiors featured in the book draw upon the styling influences and designs of Westfalia and Devon, pioneers and innovators in camping interior layouts and fittings, and seamlessly blend ideas inspired by these, and others, with imaginative personal touches and contemporary twists.

Of course, interior design is not just about layout, furniture shape and cabinet finish. One very straightforward way to transform an interior is to simply clean and refurbish the existing cabinet work, and use new fabrics and materials for seats and curtains, or even

RIGHT: A hinged, swivel table, as on this Westfalia Continental, was an excellent, flexible, space-saver.
BELOW: The Westfalia Berlin had the kitchen unit sited under the windows, and used plaids matched to the bus' exterior colours.

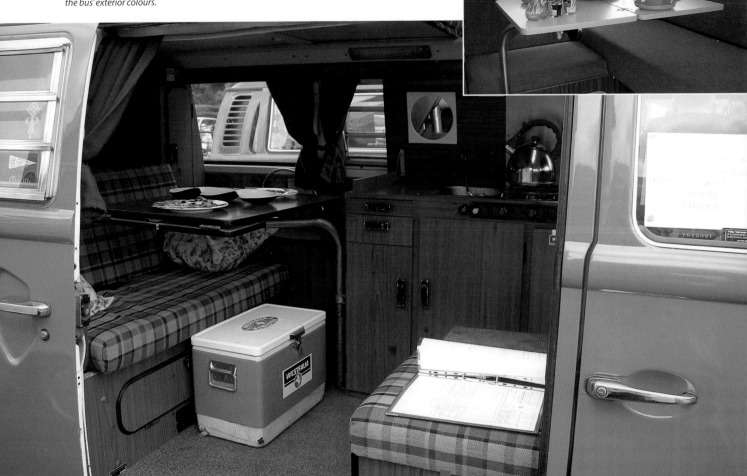

ABOVE: *The interior of this 2002 T4 Westfalia Camper shows how styling and colours have changed over time.*

RIGHT: *This 1968 Danbury shows another idea, with a pop-up cooker sited in the seat base.*

interior panels or headliner. By introducing modern or retro-style fabrics and patterns, adding contrast panels, stitching or piping detailing to upholstery, dressing the bus with accessories from throws and cushions to colour co-ordinated crockery, and being imaginative in choice of colours, a conventional or stock interior can be dramatically changed at much less effort or cost.

The title of the book says it all, really: here is a collection of inspirational interiors to enjoy looking at and to be inspired by.

Early Westfalia interiors had birch-ply roof headlining, as in this SO 34 model, which has white cabinet work.

cutting edge custom
1956 Kombi

Stuart Day's custom 1956 Kombi took the bus scene to new extremes when his street custom look made its debut in 2005: it took many awards, including the prestigious 'Volksworld Best Interior'. The hard-edged look created on the outside – with rakish stance, satin-finish Dove Blue under Off-White paint, and chromed safaris and pop-out windows, complete with 2.3 motor and black Empi 5 spokes – continues into the cab with chrome detailing of original fittings and window frames, Simpson racing harnesses and a Gene Berg shifter. However, this is in complete contrast with the light, clean flowing lines, soft curves and luxurious feel of its innovative interior living space.

Knowing that he wanted something a bit radical, Stuart called in Simon Weitz of Interior Motive, whose ground-breaking, one-off designs have caused a sensation in the world of interior conversions. Stuart outlined his ideas – for a start, the bus was to be used as a day van for relaxing in, and not for sleeping or cooking, and should have plenty of storage. He wanted something that was both cutting edge and retro modern, and which paid homage to the 1950s US diner style

ABOVE: Curved units make for a soft look, which maximizes the use of interior space.

LEFT: Soft, flowing curves and clean lines are the distinctive features of this interior.

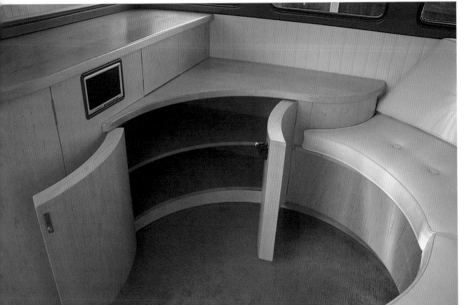

ABOVE: The section across the bulkhead is arranged on two levels, giving shelf/table space.
LEFT: A DVD player and PlayStation are fitted discreetly in the bulkhead section.

with curves, not straight lines and sharp angles. Finally he wanted a decent sound system and play station/DVD.

Simon sketched out some ideas based round a circular open space in the van, and with Stuart, firmed up what the basic shape was to be. To give the effect of a continuous curve, separate sections match seamlessly, starting with a section behind the bulkhead for the play station screen and to provide storage with the table top/shelf. Flowing from this under the windows is a curved section of lower height, with cupboards under and more table-

top space, which then turns into a curved lounge unit that runs from under the windows and across the rear, round to the load door.

Getting the curves to flow, and the back seat aligned to ensure comfortable seating, took a lot of careful thinking through, but the end result is stunning. To keep all the interior lines and surfaces smooth, Simon used push-lock cupboard doors, with no visible handles or catches. The cabinets have been built from maple, with solid wood for all the tops and maple-veneered panels, and the bottom of the unit has been finished with inset stainless-steel trim,

ABOVE: Shelves maximize storage space in the units.
BELOW: The three separate sections match seamlessly to give the effect of a continuous curve. Relaxation in comfort is what this interior is about, hence no table is needed.

The cushions in the rear are finished with a button effect for that living-room settee look.

with matching trim across the cargo door. Under the rear seat is more storage, an inverter, and a planned outlet for a Webasaco petrol heater. The play station/DVD is all wireless operated (no spaghetti of leads), and the speakers and CD stereo system are hidden in the roof unit (which has been trimmed to blend into the headliner and match the rear upper panel covering).

Many of Simon's interiors receive the finishing touches from Bernard Newbury, a name synonymous with quality and award-winning interior trimming – and this bus is no exception. The seat upholstery has been finished in a grained white leather-look vinyl (to match the exterior colour and coordinate with the maple wood), with a button finish for a softer, front-room settee look. In keeping with the clean, unbroken interior lines there are no visible fixings on the door, which have been given a vertical pleated pattern.

ABOVE: Additional storage is provided under the rear seating.

LEFT: To keep the lines clean there are no visible handles; instead, push-lock cupboard doors make for unbroken, curving lines.

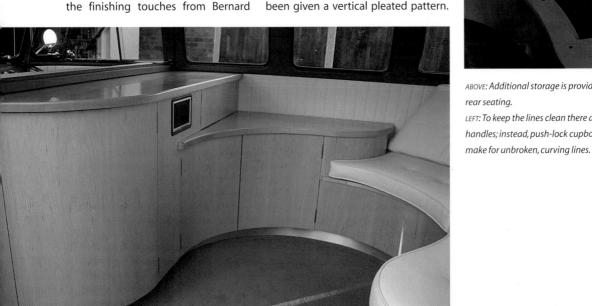

LEFT: *Racing harnesses, Gene Berg shifter and chrome detailing give a street-rod look in the cab.*

BELOW: *The units were built up around an intricate frame.*

The same vinyl is used for the cab seats, which also have the pleated pattern stitched in to contrast with the button effect in the rear. The look is set off with blue carpeting, coordinated with the exterior Dove Blue, in both cab and living area.

This is a bus designed for sitting and relaxing, a family living room that can travel to the beach or a show, and is designed as somewhere to chill out and feel comfortable. The curves have maximized the use of space, and simultaneously create the illusion of more space, whilst the use of pale colour wood and fabrics brings in more light. Freed from the restraints of a full camping interior, the end result is something hard on the outside but soft in the centre.

LEFT: *The cab area both contrasts with and complements the living area, whilst pleated side and door panels provide unity of styling.*

BELOW: *The cab seat has a pleated finish to contrast with the lounge seating.*

starting afresh
1964 Split Screen Camper

LEFT: A full-width bulkhead unit, finished in maple, discreetly contains a cooker, sink and fridge. The large open run of worktop doubles as a shelf or table.

BELOW: A Waeco portable fridge and waste-water container are sited under the circular stainless-steel sink with electric pump tap.

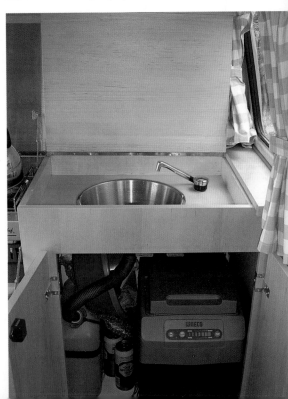

This 1964 camper was originally a Devon Caravette. It had been lovingly restored to a high standard before Andrew and Krissy Spencer acquired it, and featured a fully refurbished Caravette interior complete with original upholstery and curtains. The bus had been upgraded for today's road conditions with 1641cc engine, creative IRS and bay front beam and discs, and the exterior had been given period custom styling with chrome safari windows, cab window surrounds and pop-outs to complement the new pastel blue and light grey paint scheme.

Although the Devon interior was in superb condition it really did not suit Andrew and Krissy's needs. Whilst the period design has a charm of its own, the bed is a fiddle to lay out (and uncomfortable unless you are less than six foot tall), the cooker not very efficient, and the evaporation coolbox really does not keep things at safe temperatures. They agonized for ages over the stock versus custom, originality

LEFT: Subtle exterior pastel colours are carried through to the spacious interior, which is set off with period-style black and white floor tiles.

versus functionality issues, but ultimately needed something they could actually use. With the children now grown up, they wanted an interior they could use for weekends away, as well as touring in the UK and abroad. They wanted a sense of space and light, and needed to be able to eat and sleep comfortably and have enough storage for all the camping paraphernalia. Plus there had to be room for the labrador to sleep on the floor if the awning was not erected. The Devon interior, period perfect as it was, simply did not meet their requirements, and so, after much soul searching, it was stripped out and a loving new home found for it.

In designing a replacement interior there were several key issues to address. The layout had to be more user friendly; an easy-action bed had to be roomy and accommodate a six-footer; and the interior had to be light and airy with no full-length cupboards/wardrobes or dark finishing. This has all been achieved using just three basic units finished in maple: a bulkhead storage unit with built-in sink and cooker, a full-width rear seat/rock-and-roll bed, and a roof locker.

Having stripped out the Devon interior and the internal door cards, Andrew set about attending to any rust, painting and wax-oiling before fully insulating the bus with 1in-thick solid insulation foam and sound insulation damping. A new TMI interior panel set, finished in light grey with a

ABOVE: The end cupboard makes an excellent kitchen larder. A colour coordinated crockery set and period radio add to the overall effect.
BELOW: The bulkhead cabinet is angled at the front to create space and draw in the eye. Stitched TMI interior panels in grey set the base tone for the interior colour scheme.

ABOVE: *A light, airy interior has been achieved with light grey interior panels, cream upholstery and blue/ white gingham curtains. Persian-style mat and scatter cushions bring in colour and a sense of opulence.*

ABOVE: *The cupboards under the cooker are shelved to maximize kitchen storage space.*
RIGHT: *The modern cooker/grill has more hob space, and the housing and lid are lined in stainless steel for heat protection/ hygiene.*

horizontal stitch pattern, sets a soothing and neutral tone, and cab seats were recovered to match in grey vinyl with lighter grey centre sections, stitching detail and white piped edges by Spirit of the Fifties. After much searching they finally found a local cabinet maker, Renzo Rapaccioli, to build the bulkhead unit to their design specifications. Finished in maple laminate for a clean modern look, the unit angles in to create open space at the doorway and runs across the full width providing a large shelf/work-top area.

The shelved section by the door is a large storage cupboard, a twin hob/ grill unit is sited in the middle (with gas bottle and storage under), and next to the window is an electric pump tap and circular stainless-steel sink, with fresh and waste water containers, and a Waeco 12V/240V refrigerator sited in the base. Cabinet work is double-faced MDF in maple, which has been sprayed inside and out with a semi-matt varnish for a hardwearing finish. The cooker and sink are accessed from flip-up hinged lids, and the cooker compartment and lid are finished inside in protective stainless steel. A full-width Bluebird Customs rock-and-roll bed with matching maple finish base and a roof locker add additional storage. A set of mounted flush push-button handles adds to the contemporary look, and the addition of 240V hook-up and Kenwood CD

ABOVE: The rear area has been left open with no side cupboards, to develop the airy feeling of space.
LEFT: Additional storage is in an enclosed roof locker and rear seat base, both finished in maple to match the bulkhead unit.

receiver with Focal speakers makes for comfortable, on-site camping.

The seating/bed cushions are memory foam covered in a cream, rough-weave Irish linen fabric from John Lewis. Linen gingham fabric, also from John Lewis, has been used for the curtains, and the blue and white check pattern both harmonizes with the exterior and interior colours, and adds to the airy feel; while Persian-style scatter cushions and mats are a reminder of Andrew's time as a young man spent living in Iran, and bring in contrasting

colour. The rear area has been kept open to keep the sense of space and light, and there is plenty of floor area for the dog to stretch out on, with a hint of Devon heritage coming from the classic check pattern black and white floor tiles.

Whilst some may baulk at stripping out a period interior, Andrew and Krissy have ended up with something classy and practical that fits their needs, meaning that it is used as was originally intended, as opposed to becoming just a showpiece. They set

out to achieve an uncomplicated, functional interior; there was no over-arching design plan or styling theme as such. The resulting understated mix of light and pastel shades that unifies the whole look, is both modern and period. Greys and blues blend and harmonize subtly, making for an interior that is roomy, light, comfortable and eminently practical and stylish.
(Photographs courtesy of Andrew Spencer)

RIGHT: The full-width roof locker has circular stick-on LED lights.
BELOW: Harmonizing grey tones are carried through in the cab, including finishing details such as the horn push and two-tone grey cab seats. A bud vase adds period styling, and the Madonna of the Highway watches serenely over travellers.

tangerine dream
1976 Bespoke Bay

ABOVE: The sunroof allows light to pour in, creating a warm orange glow in this stylish modern interior.

LEFT: The interior has been finished predominantly in orange, with white detailing, to match the exterior. Maple cabinets and flooring lighten the interior. Note the speaker grills cut into the seat base.

Although this 1976 bay started life as a Devon camper, by the time John Shepherd acquired it nothing of that heritage remained. However, the body had been fully restored and repainted in Brilliant Orange under Pearl White, a Paris Beetles' sunroof had been fitted to replace the pop top, and all the mechanics and running gear had been overhauled and refurbished. A bus in this excellent condition, with an empty inside ready for an interior, suited John perfectly, as it meant he could start from scratch to create something personal and striking, but also fully equipped for family camping.

To be used as a full-on camper meant the works: cooker, sink, fridge, storage, dining and seating for four, and a roomy bed. The first decision was that the rear seat/rock-and-roll bed would be full width, meaning the facilities would have to be somehow sited behind the front seats. He wanted a bright, clean look that would draw on traditional designs but also incorporate ideas of his own, and, after working up some scale drawings, contacted Vaughn and Tim of Classic, Custom and Retro after a recommendation from Adam at the Old Volks Home. Together they sat down and discussed in detail how John's ideas could actually be

ABOVE: Extra storage is in the pelmet cupboards that run to meet the roof locker.

ABOVE: The full-width rock-and-roll bed takes up two-thirds of the interior, providing ample space for sleeping in comfort.

made to work and incorporated, and with their expertise and advice the final design was drawn up, and then built.

John wanted to use the orange exterior colour to set the interior theme by having seats and cushions upholstered to match. He chose maple-veneered ply over maple frames for the cabinet work, as the pale colour of the wood would harmonize with the bright seating and form a subtle background. With no room for side cabinets, two units

have been built that sit on either side of the gangway, and make ingenious use of the limited space left after the fitting of a full-width bed.

The unit by the load door contains the cooker and grill with stainless-steel windshield, with utensil drawer and storage cupboard. Based on the designs pioneered by Devon in 1965, this self-contained unit swings out and can also be lifted out entirely for use in an awning, or to free up interior space. The unit behind the driver is a single

ABOVE: A small, portable buddy seat provides additional storage and seating at the table.

BELOW: A full-width rear seat bed makes for a spacious interior. Orange/white check curtains coordinate with the upholstery; the table is of maple.

ABOVE: *The units on either side of the gangway contain cooker, fridge, sink, storage and a single seat. The light maple wood harmonizes with the upholstery, and stainless-steel push-button handles keep the modern styling theme.*

ABOVE: *The self-contained cooker unit, based on the 1960s Devon design, swings out for use outside, and is also fully demountable for use in an awning, creating more space inside when camped up.*

A top-loading, removable fridge is sited in the base of the rear-facing single seat.

seat, in the base of which is sited a removable, top-loading mains/12V/gas fridge, which is more convenient and takes up less space than a fridge in a unit of its own. Being removable means it can also be used in the awning, where the facility to run off gas comes into its own. A pump-tap stainless-steel sink unit, with hinged lid and splashback, has been sited at the rear of this seat, with the water container in a cupboard directly underneath. Another of John's ideas was for pelmet storage cupboards that run above the side windows to meet the roof unit at the rear, creating plenty of additional storage. LED lighting in the rear adds another personal touch.

A small enclosed buddy seat provides yet more storage, and sits in the gangway when travelling, or at the table to provide dinette-style seating for four. The table is mounted traditionally on the side wall, but is also finished in maple with a modern chrome leg. There is a matching detachable extension that creates a full-width table for extra dining comfort. Steel push-button handles on the furniture make for a contemporary look, whilst custom door and window handles in the cab add a bit of street style. Driving in comfort is as important as camping in comfort to John, hence the addition of Porsche 944 seats with headrests, trimmed to match the panels and rear seat cushions, up front.

ABOVE: A sink has been cleverly sited behind the single seat.

RIGHT: Interior panels have been finished to match the seats, with pleated lower sections separated by white piping and twin white stripes.

The upholstery has been done in orange vinyl with white detailing to match the exterior paintwork, which also harmonizes well with the maple cabinets and maple laminate flooring. The interior panels, cab seats and rear seats all have white piping, twin white stripes and stitching detail to enhance the overall look, and coordinating, small check, orange and white curtains make for a unified colour palette.

On a sunny day, light just pours in and creates a warm, orange glow in this stylish interior. The clever use of space makes for a roomy and airy interior, which still has all the facilities and storage necessary for camping in comfort, including a Propex heater.

LEFT: The orange and white colour scheme has been carried through into the cab, including the front kick panels. Black carpet coordinates with the dashboard and door handles..

BELOW: Porsche 944 seats with headrests, trimmed to match the panels and rear seat cushions, add to the stylish modern look. The small buddy seat sits between them when travelling.

modernizing a Moonraker
1982 Devon Moonraker

It's not always necessary to start from scratch to revamp an interior, especially if the existing interior layout suits your needs and is in sound condition. This T3 Moonraker has been given a modern makeover with new cupboard doors, curtains, upholstery, flooring and personal styling touches, but the basic Devon layout has been retained.

Alan and Caroline Pritchard acquired the bus in 2006 from Tony Major of Cambridge. The original Moonraker interior, with units under the window, pull-out bed and buddy seat with folding extension leaf, was complete, albeit a bit scruffy and tired, but the exterior had been freshly repainted in Holographic Black, giving a very distinctive and up-to-the-minute look to the bus. The finish is a bit like metal flake, with a spectrum of colours that flash and shine in the sun showing glints of red, greens, blues and purples in bright sun and dominant reds when skies are greyer. It was the red tints and sparkle that actually inspired the interior colour choice, and the red/cream gingham curtains were the first item to be sourced to pick up on this colour theme, echoing the red sparkle from

ABOVE: The buddy seat can be used for storage or to accommodate a porta potti.

LEFT: The original Devon Moonraker interior has been kept but given a modern makeover, with new cupboard doors, upholstery, curtains, flooring and personal styling touches.

the exterior and the cream of the existing interior cabinet work.

The main cabinet, containing the cooker, fridge, sink and storage, was still in its original cream laminate finish and cleaned up well. The brown doors and trim made it looked dated, however, so Alan decided to replace them. He chose Astra Prim Red for the new door colours, and Truwood, in Mold, North Wales, made up each door individually for him, with all the edges finished in red. The wardrobe and roof cupboard doors have also been replaced. A matching false front has been added to the space above the fridge, making a secret compartment, and the original Devon handles were then sprayed with black plasticoat and refitted. Personal styling touches can be seen on the rear wardrobe door, which features a VW badge and pool ball handle, and in the cutlery drawer embossed with Volkswagen. The new doors bring a contemporary touch of colour to the interior, which is set off by the red and cream colour theme carried through to the upholstery.

The bench seat, rear bed cushion and buddy seat have been re-upholstered in red and cream by C. Andrews, UTS Upholstery of Flintshire, and feature red pleated centre panels and piping with the colours chosen to match

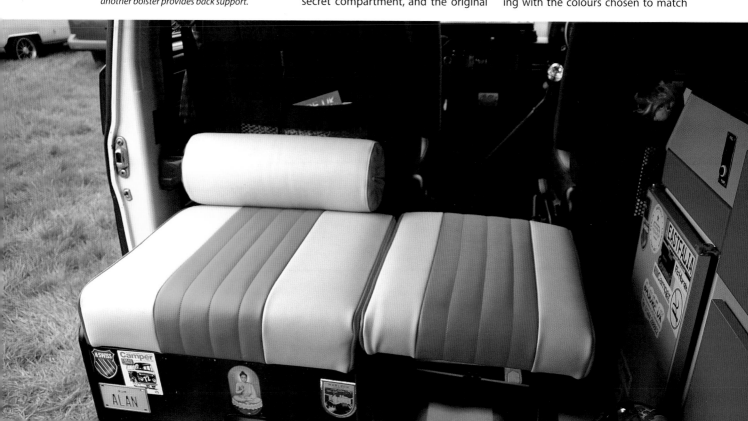

RIGHT: The original Devon leg and fittings were used to convert a skimboard into a table.

BELOW: The stylish skimboard table shape makes for easy access around it.

the red doors and cream cabinet. Co-ordinating cream bolsters, with red-buttoned end panels, add a luxurious living-room settee touch and a back support on the buddy seat. Black and white check tile-effect cushion floor recreates period styling, and the black has been followed through with soft, textured black carpet for all interior walls and panels, and black bench and buddy seat bases. Two 9 x 6 JBL speakers are mounted in the rear seat base, as is an outlet for the Propex heater (fitted by Steve at Gassure of Chester), and another personal detailing touch can be seen in an original Devon Conversions badge that sits between them. A Pioneer head unit supplies the sound, and there is also a twin-screen DVD set-up (from Maplins),

ABOVE: Red hibiscus flower transfers add to the surfing theme brought in by the table. Black and white check cushion floor adds a period styling look.
BELOW: Three spotlights have been added above the worktop.

A period radio, with red trim, makes an excellent colour-matched accessory.

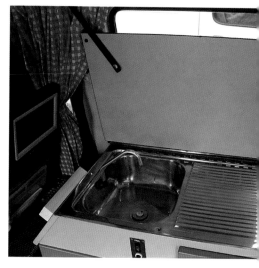

ABOVE: *The original sink still functions perfectly. Note the DVD screen mounted on the headrest back.*

ABOVE: *Details such as a black cutlery drawer embossed with Volkswagen add to the personal styling.*

with screens mounted on the cab seat headrests, and the player sited under the front passenger seat.

Three 12V spotlights (from Home-base) have been fitted above the long worktop area, and ambient lighting comes from LED strips and spots on the seat base, rear side panel and under the roof cupboard. More personal touches can be seen in the red hibiscus flower 'Air Cooled' transfer on the floor by the load door, the single red flower trans-fers on the original cream interior paint by the rear window, and the stickers that decorate the fridge and buddy seat base.

The table is a skimboard sourced at Vanwest. Alan has used the original Devon table chrome leg and mount-ings to convert this into a useful floor-mounted swivelling table, and the black design on the top also coordi-nates with the interior scheme.

Alan and Caroline have brought a whole new look to their Devon, and the modern, jazzy interior is the perfect partner for that stunning paintwork effect.

The wardrobe door has been personalized with a VW badge and pool ball handle.

the lounge
1956 Panel Van

LEFT: The side walls are lined with leather, as are the door panels, which feature shaped cowhide inserts.

BELOW: Ambient lighting is provided by flush-mounted LED lights in the roof, whilst the surfboard-style table acts as a bar.

Owner Darren Larwood describes his bus, called The Lounge, as 'total indulgence with no compromise', and he has taken interior design and concept to new heights with a luxurious interior finished in oak and trimmed in tan Italian leather and real cowhide.

Being a 1950s bus, Darren decided to go for a retro look that had Art Deco influences, and took his inspiration from the American den/lounge look and styling, with the interior built as 'chilling' area with a bar and comfortable seating. Designed as such, it has not been built for camping and sleeping, purely for fun and relaxation with friends.

As usual for a panel van, there was no interior fitted, though when Darren acquired it there was a mish-mash of old Bay Westfalia parts and home-made pieces, and a tatty old blue carpet on the floor. Before any work could start on the interior the body required major attention, as there was extensive rot from the centre chassis right through to the front! Darren then set about sketching ideas with friend Pooch, who was going to build all the interior seating and cabinets, to include practical storage space, subtle lighting, a bar, and a discretely hidden sound system. To maximize living space, they

ABOVE: *Mellow oak, Texan Longhorn cowhide, tan Italian leather and cream faux suede work in harmony, making for a luxurious and decadent interior.*

ABOVE: *The seat bases are made from solid oak with leather inserts in the centre sections.*
BELOW: *The seats are trimmed in tan leather with genuine cowhide insert panels. Note the polished aluminium matching detailing of the table inserts, table leg, speaker outlet surrounds and armrest knobs.*

opted for the classic twin bench seats round a flap-down table layout – though as can be seen from the photos, this would upturn conventional arrangements! Darren also decided the interior would be built from oak for that classic period look, combined with leather and cowhide for luxury and uniqueness.

Style and individuality are the key concepts that underpin this interior, with the colours and materials complementing each other perfectly. The floor and rear cargo area have been fitted with solid oak, interior panels are in Italian tan leather, and the headlining is cream faux suede. One of the eye-

catching features is the use of real Texan Longhorn cowhide, in brown and white to harmonize with the floor, panels and headlining, as centre sections for cab and rear seats. Darren's partner, Jo Filer-Cooper, did all the upholstery, carrying out some very tricky work following the curve on the seating, and shaping and saddle stitching the leather and cowhide to fit around the panels. Jo's attention to detail can be seen in the shaped cowhide inserts on cab and load door panels, and the use of cowhide on the rear cabinet and roof locker doors.

The seats themselves have been designed and built for lounging in

comfort, and exude decadence, with deep curves, curved oak armrests, and the use of wood mixed with leather on the covered base and end sections. Speakers have also been mounted in the rear-facing seat base, with additional speakers in the rear cabinets behind the front-facing seat. In keeping with the striking design and the surfing culture that is associated with the VW bus, the table itself is a work of art: built from oak and shaped like a surfboard with a polished ally pedestal leg, it doubles as a bar with four polished aluminium inserts designed specifically to hold beer bottles! When not in use it clips to the sidewall, creating more floor space. Another classy detailing touch is the use of a darker oak centre section (giving a stripe effect) that both harmonizes and contrasts with all the interior colours.

Originally the amps were to be kept in the roof locker, but concerns over heat dissipation led to them being sited out in the open on the back of the rear seat. The sound system itself is a Vibe twin 12in sub enclosure with twin amps and component speakers powered by a head unit sited in the rear cupboard. Finishing touches are provided by

ABOVE: The polished ally detailing theme is continued in the cab with the door handles and gear knob. Note the different shaped cowhide inserts for the cab doors.

bespoke aluminium buttons on the wood armrest tops, knobs and door handles, speaker outlet surrounds, as well as the surround for the flush-mounted LED lights in the cargo roof and in the rear.

Outside, the theme has been kept simple, with classic matt Dove Blue paint and some very cool traditional signwriting. A full-length roof rack, single roof-mounted spotlight, OG 15in polished Fuchs and a serious lowering job complete the street look, which combines period and custom styling. Darren would like to thank Jo for her design and upholstery skills, and also Pooch (www.pointblankpixels.com), who did all the woodwork including

seating, cupboards, floor, and all interior panels as well as fitting the sound system. Together these three have created a bus that certainly causes a stir wherever it goes!

The bus still works for a living, in keeping with its past: Darren and Jo also run a VW wedding hire business, and The Lounge is often used as wedding transport with its ambient lighting, cool sounds, cold beers and sumptuous interior, making that special day even more special.

(Find out more about wedding hire and their other buses available on www.vweddinghire.com.)
(Photographs courtesy of Pooch, and Darren Larwood)

ABOVE: The front bench seat is trimmed in leather and cowhide to match.

RIGHT: The rear area has a panelled oak base to match the floor, and twin storage units. It is also where the amps have been sited.

production prototype
1972 Bespoke Camper Conversion

The original 1972 hand-built interior in this camper was designed to go into production, but the untimely death of the retired aircraft engineer who was planning to set up his new business meant that only two were ever produced. The interior is exceptionally well thought out to provide masses of storage space, and has many novel touches and ideas not often seen.

The bus actually started life as a Pastel White panel van, and was built in July 1972. Most panel van conversions use side windows that are flush with the body, but the windows fitted were sourced from VW and are completely

different, being shaped with a recessed frame detail and highly polished.

The interior itself is finished to a very high standard. Inspired by Devon for style and light oak finish, every inch of space has been carefully thought through to maximize storage space and flexibility of use. The entire rear area has been panelled in soft white vinyl.

Behind the passenger seat to the left of the sliding door entrance is an oak unit containing the sink with whale pump and hinged Formica top, waste pipe and storage underneath for the water and waste containers. It also has

ABOVE: A low-back single seat, with storage under, is sited behind the driver.
RIGHT: The woodwork is all hand-finished in light oak, with storage in every conceivable area of space; the whole rear interior has been panelled in soft white vinyl.

ABOVE: The interior design has been carefully thought through to maximize space. The table has had the sharp corners removed to make for easier access, and the floor unit can be accessed from the front or the top.

ABOVE: A folding plate drainer is fitted inside the top of the cooker lid, which can be used when it is in the 'up' position. Next to the cooker unit is another Formica-topped hinged cupboard where a convenient plastic waste bin is kept.

LEFT: Drawers in the cooker unit contain the utensils and crockery. There is even a built-in wine bottle holder!

BELOW: There are more drawers behind the rear seat back.

two smaller cupboards for plates and other crockery, and a small drawer where the original cutlery is still kept, in mint condition.

By the side of the rear seat there is a cabinet for the double-ring cooker, in excellent, original, almost unused condition, with a Formica hinged top with a folding plate drainer inside the top that can be used when it is in the 'up' position; more storage cupboards, and another drawer for salt and pepper, and cups and glasses. Behind this there is yet another Formica hinged-top cupboard with the original, correct size, plastic waste bin in it.

Behind the rear double seat there are two deep side units in oak, the offside being a small wardrobe unit for hanging shirts and jackets, on the nearside a full height storage cupboard, and at the rear of this the spare wheel. Between the two is an oak overhead storage area, under which the Formica-

BELOW: The original cutlery supplied with the camper is still intact, and the quality of the workmanship can be seen in touches such as the green baize lining for the cutlery drawer.

ABOVE: A solid oak cabinet sited by the load door contains pump tap and sink with cutlery drawer and plenty of storage space.

RIGHT: Water and waste containers are kept under the sink, with easy access via a side door.

BELOW: The sink unit has a hinged Formica top with bowl and drainer area.

topped oak table slides for storage when not in use (a feature pioneered by Devon in the 1950s).

Between the two side cupboards over the engine bay there is a chest of two drawers on the left-hand side, with a matching pair of drawers accessible from the tailgate, and a storage chest from front to back with a hinged top. All cupboards and the table-top storage track have a rotary oak retaining catch.

Under the rear seat is storage for the table leg and the two oak veneer bed sections: these clip into place between the seat behind the driver's seat frame and the walk-through area, to make up part of the base of the double bed. Between the rear double seat and the single seat along the offside wall there is a three-section, folding, low-level storage cupboard top in Formica/oak that also makes up the rest of the bed, with all four seat cushions making the mattress. There is additional storage under the single seat that now contains a leisure battery, split charger and fuse box, with ventilation holes cut into the oak base.

Paul Dodd acquired the camper, still in near-perfect condition, in 2006, and

since owning it, has carried out some subtle modifications and upgrades that are fully in keeping with a period look. These include changing the original optional front fog lamps to a period NOS circular type with yellow tint, adding Deluxe alloy trim to the front air intake grille, and fitting new stainless-steel wipers, restoring the original 14in steel wheels by painting them in Kansas Beige (correct for the year), and adding stainless-steel rings, split bus/1968–70 Bay domed hubcaps, and Wolfsburg valve caps. Other extras now include jailbars, Safety Star light, leisure battery and 12V outlets in the side of the seat base and in the dash for the SatNav. A modern retro-style CD/MP3 player sits discretely in the dash, with the speakers mounted in the front kick panels to avoid cutting the door panels.

(Photographs courtesy of Julian Hunt)

ABOVE: Apart from a discrete stereo unit, the cab is as it was over thirty-five years ago, with all the original upholstery in pristine condition.

BELOW: At the back is a closed storage unit, with open storage under the right side cabinet, which can also be accessed from the front. Note how the back of the left side unit has been shaped to accommodate the spare wheel.

BELOW: The rear luggage area contains a twin unit comprising drawers and lidded storage box.

red hot
1965 Custom Kombi

BELOW: Ice bucket, champagne and cocktail glasses delicately detailed with red recreate the period look of luxury and elegance.

The bulkhead unit contains the Blaupunkt amp set-up.

ABOVE: A free-standing Blaupunkt 750-watt sub-woofer delivers some serious sound! Matching accessories, such as coordinated scatter cushions and red and white mugs, all help to create an elegant and unified look.

This 1965 Australian import Split is full-on cutting-edge custom, built for looks and speed but with a sumptuous interior that mixes 1950s kitsch with decadent luxury. Owners Andy and Deanna Jones spent two years creating this look, and the end result is something that exceeds all expectations!

The outside is finished in House of Color Kandy Apple Red over Orion Silver base, with Old English White for the upper body. This pearlescent-effect paint shimmers and changes hues according to the light, and in sunshine the finish sparkles and gleams. The street stance has been achieved by fitting a Creative Engineering weed-eater front beam and IRS with adjustable spring plates, dropped spindles, CSP disc brakes, front and rear safaris, polished stainless-steel bumpers and chromed Fuchs alloys. A 1776cc performance engine and Rancho Pro-Street Special Freeway Flyer gearbox

LEFT: A full-width rear settee, with centre panels of quilted red Alacantra fabric and with sumptuous end cushions, creates opulent living space. Speakers are built into the padded seat/bed base.

BELOW: The bulkhead unit, finished in walnut burr laminate with dark wood trim, recreates the style of a 1950s curved cocktail cabinet.

ABOVE: More speakers are built into the matching roof cabinet, which also contains the head units.

BELOW: The interior is light, airy and spacious, and the matching walnut roof unit sits unobtrusively above the cocktail cabinet.

maximize cruising ability at higher speeds, meaning the bus can travel comfortably at 70mph (112km/h) on the motorway. Andy had decided on the tech specs and exterior look, so Deanna set about designing an interior that would be as distinctive as the outside.

They already had a Bay camper for family camping, but the Split offered the chance to create something for themselves to use and enjoy. Released from the need to design a camping interior, as they always used an awning for cooking and washing, they were free to design something radical. Deanna's design plan started with a Creative full-width rock-and-roll bed and, for maximum floor space, a storage unit that would run across the width of the front bulkhead with a matching roof cupboard above. Taking a 1950s style

ABOVE: Kick panel and door panel and seat inserts are quilted to match the cab headliner and sun visors. Note touches such as the banjo steering wheel, stainless-steel gas pedal, switches, wiper stalk, grab and door pull handles and bud vase complete with matching red gerbera.

BELOW: The side door panels are trimmed in cream vinyl with quilted red fabric centre sections to match the interior design.

Attention to detail is everywhere in this bus: from cushions to ornaments, everything has been carefully chosen to blend and complement the interior design.

cocktail cabinet as the theme, she drew out a detailed sketch plan for a unit with a curved end that would fit both a cocktail cabinet and a DVD player. A local joinery company, Fileturn of Bristol, built the furniture to this design, and to recreate the 1950s cocktail cabinet period look, walnut burr laminate has been used to face the units, with dark wood edging flush to all edges. Above this is a matching roof unit, with the door hinged to face the rear, where the sound system head units and additional speakers are sited.

Having seen the quality of interior trimming carried out by Steve of SJ Bowles Interiors, they knew he could turn their ambitious ideas into reality. They wanted the interior scheme to be finished in a classy red and cream to complement the exterior colours, and after much discussion and sample checking, opted for cream vinyl as the base colour, with soft red Alacantra fabric for contrasting detail and adding a touch of classy luxury. Steve suggested refinements such as the quilted red inserts to the seats and side panels, the

BELOW: The rear seat is also a roomy rock-and-roll bed, which is quick and easy to convert.

AVOVE: The quilted inserts in the front panels follow the lines of the cab door.

BELOW: Additional gauges are mounted in the air-intake vent to preserve clean dash lines, and the cab headliner and sun visors are quilted to match the interior.

matching quilted headliner and sun visors in the cab, and the stainless-steel interior pull handles. His attention to practical detail can be seen in the matching lift-out German square-weave carpets with overlocked edges, and cab mats that have non-slip rubber sections sewn in.

The custom look has been carried through into the cab with a banjo steering wheel, Scat shifter and stainless-steel gas pedal, light switches, indicator-stalk dash grab handle and bud vase.

Deanna is known to her family as the 'accessory queen', and she has set about sourcing items to dress the bus for maximum impact at shows, including period ice bucket and champagne,

red-patterned cocktail glasses, matching scatter cushions, red and white patterned mugs, red gerbera flowers in a steel dash bud vase and glass vase, even a display of bright jelly beans next to a photo of a Split marooned on an ice floe. These finishing details dress the bus and present it dramatically, making it a confirmed crowd pleaser at shows.

Andy's dream was to simply turn up at a show, open the side doors and play some 'banging tunes'. As you might expect, the ICE is also a bit special and features a Blaupunkt Memphis MP66 head unit, two Blaupunkt 1600-watt four-way amps, four 360-watt two-component speakers and tweeters, and a 750-watt sub-woofer!

BELOW: The cab seats are trimmed to match the rear seat and interior panels, and coordinating red carpet covers the bulkhead and continues under the seats.

rock and roll bay
1972 Rock Music-Themed Camper

With so many different styles of interior around, it is hard to come up with something radically new. So the starting point for Craig and Caroline Robinson was to choose a theme and design a practical interior around that. The camper had to be used for its original purpose, but it also had to be something to be admired and enjoyed by others. Given Craig's passion for music, it seemed only natural that a rock/guitar theme should be chosen as the starting point.

Their 1972 bus was by now tired and worn, with old-fashioned curtains and carpets, an ancient bed that was really awkward to set up, and no modern extras such as a hook-up to power Craig's iPod collection – so they started by simply stripping everything out. Taking the bus's black-and-white exterior colour scheme, they decided to carry this through to the interior and use modern materials to make something very striking and contemporary. They then spent a lot of time in the bus thinking of ideas and sketching out how things might look and fit, with practicality and impact being the watchwords. The bus had to be usable as a camper, so storage, portaloo, fridge and cooking facilities were needed – but Craig also wanted modern lighting and electrics to power a decent sound system that could connect to his iPod.

As everyone knows, space is at a premium in the VW bus, and any interior will inevitably mean some compromises

ABOVE: Units have been built using white ash with gloss black cabinet doors and tops, sourced from a kitchen design centre. Industrial metal check plate flooring adds an urban look.
LEFT: The interior has been styled round a rock music theme, with a black and white colour scheme chosen to coordinate with the exterior paintwork.

ABOVE: The rear seat/pull-out bed has been upholstered in leather-look vinyl using a button effect, with black shaggy fabric cushions to tie in with the colour scheme.

RIGHT: The rock theme has been developed by the use of Marshall logos and amplifier-style handles on all cabinets, with touches such as a Sticky Fingers sticker, Hendrix print and gig tickets 'fly posted' on walls.

and trade-offs. Initial plans for a sink were soon discarded – it would take up a lot of space, and washing in a bowl is actually more practical than using a small sink in a confined space! Having decided on a basic layout of units on each side of the gangway, storage on either side of a pull-out bed, and a removable buddy seat where the porta potti could be kept, Craig then carefully measured items such as toilets and fridges to see what available items would fit best, and to allow him to make the most of the available space left when they were in place.

Then it was time to start the actual build. White ash frames with gloss black doors and surface tops (from Cottage Bedrooms of Beverley) were chosen to mirror the exterior and create a

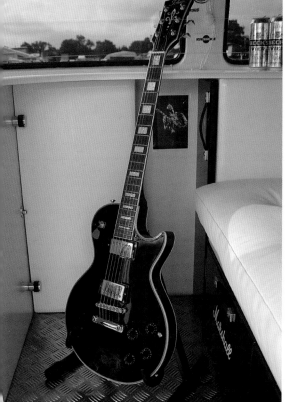

ABOVE: A free-standing buddy seat, upholstered to match the rear seat, has been designed to look like an amplifier and contains a porta potti. Retro-style, swirly pattern curtains are fitted in the cab and rear window.

LEFT: A classic Gibson Les Paul replica guitar, finished in black to maintain the interior design's colour unity, provides a classy finishing touch to the rock music styling of the interior.

stylish modern and striking look, with metal check plate for flooring, and a cooker shield for that urban, industrial feel. It was sometimes a case of 'adapt and improve' as the build took shape, and some units had to be rebuilt and some doors resized to fit! Craig also designed and built his own pull-out bed system, which took a lot of trial and error to get right. Additional extra storage is provided under the seat.

The porta potti is stored in a specially built single seat, upholstered to match the rear seat, designed to resemble an amplifier cabinet. The side wall under and above the windows opposite the load door has also been faced with white ash, and the top of the unit that contains the fridge curves back to form a shelf that runs under the windows and meets the storage unit at the side of the rear seat where the power management system is installed.

White leather-look vinyl has been chosen to upholster the seating using a modern sofa button design, with shaggy fabric scatter cushions in black to match the cabinet doors. Marshall logos and amplifier handles for the cabinets set the rock-and-roll guitar tone, and

ABOVE: *The cooker and kitchen storage unit is sited by the load door behind the front passenger seat. Metal check plate, matching the floor, has been used to face the inside areas to provide insulation and a windshield round the cooker.*

RIGHT: *A Waeco fridge, with storage above, is sited in the cabinet behind the driver.*

Chrome strip lights double as hanging rails, and roller blinds have been fitted to the side windows to keep an uncluttered look in the interior.

details such as the small pictures of gig tickets, rock icons such as Hendrix and the Sticky Fingers logo add to the overall effect. When on show, all this is set off with a classic black finish Gibson Les Paul replica guitar on display.

Neat finishing details include model buses, steel-finish electric fan and chrome waste bin and the chrome wall lights that double as hanging rails and which were sourced from a major DIY chainstore. Roller blinds have been used for the side windows instead of curtains, which means no flapping fabric hang-

ing down to detract from the overall effect, and the browny red colour in the retro-style, swirly pattern fabric of the front and rear curtains has been matched in the red roller blind fabric.

Then, of course, there is the music system. A Pioneer head unit and iPod dock pump up the volume via the twin speaker cabinet sited at the side of the rear seat; after all, a rock-and-roll theme bus needs ear-bleeding sound to be true to its heritage!

(Additional photographs courtesy of Craig Robinson)

43

9

Devon makeover
1968 Devon Caravette

ABOVE: New upholstery in beige/cream/brown with a button finish, and a slatted door on the cooker unit, modernize the interior look.

BELOW: All the doors and panels, originally faced with grey-white melamine, have been replaced with wood versions.

The original character and styling of the Devon interior and its polished oak cabinets has been preserved. Modern styling has been brought in with new fabrics, floor tiles, wood panelling, and wood cabinet doors that add to the natural look of the interior.

Rather than a radical redesign, another route is to renovate and modernize an existing interior, whilst keeping in sympathy with the original conversion. This is especially so if the existing interior is basically in reasonable condition. This 1968 Devon Caravette does exactly that, owners Ant and Emma having decided they would update the interior on their Devon themselves by adding and changing things to create a retro-modern look that was in keeping with original Devon styling, but which incorporated their own personal touches.

The original Caravette interior that came with the camper was intact and complete, but in a very worn condition, with a heavily nicotine-stained headlining, a cooker that looked as if it was last cleaned in 1968, and what Ant describes as 'curtains and cushions finished in the loudest material known to man'. From the outset they decided that any revamping would keep the original character and styling of the Devon

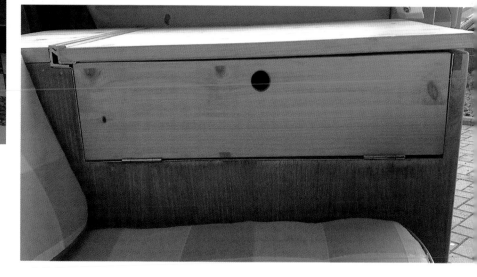

ABOVE: *The roof has been panelled in wood to match the new panelling round the seat bases. Matching new curtains, tiebacks and upholstery sit alongside original period features such as the bed.*

ABOVE: *The twin single seats have had the backs made shorter so as not to break the cab and living spaces. Devon-style reversible cushions have been made up with grey vinyl and a modern open plaid that harmonizes with the grey interior panels and exterior Savannah Beige paintwork.*

ABOVE: *Wood top and front sections for the cooker housing replace the original melamine versions. Finger holes mean no protrusions to catch on.*

BELOW: *Original polished oak woodwork has been sanded back, and wood panelling fitted to seat bases. The original water-tank filling system has been retained.*

interior, and that the oak cabinets and basic layout would be preserved. Variations on the theme would come from new tiles, wood panelling, and new doors and handles that would add to the natural look of the light oak interior.

One of the first things they wanted to change was to include a sink, as the original Caravette had only a pump tap (a sink was optional equipment!). Having sourced a sink with a 12V pumped water supply from a T25, they decided to locate this in the buddy seat base, and Ant also lowered the height of both single seat backs by 5cm to make the cab and living areas feel more unified. The other single seat is now home to an amplifier, fitted against the bulk-

head behind the back section. The cabinets themselves were just sanded back to a lighter finish, and wooden panelling installed on the vertical surfaces such as the buddy seat and bench seat bases. The doors were all recut from wood, and all cabinet top surfaces replaced, and a modern-style, slatted door was fitted to the front of the unit that contains the cooker, giving access to the gas bottle. Finger holes were cut into the door fronts to avoid protrusions in seating areas, and a classy modern styling detail is the use of stainless-steel cupboard handles shaped like chillis. The original cooker was simply cleaned, stripped and refurbished, using copious amounts of

ABOVE: *Chilli-shaped stainless-steel handles have been fitted to all the new wooden doors, including the roof locker. The original cooker with folding windshield and plate rack has been cleaned and renovated to keep an authentic period feel.*

LEFT: *The table top has been covered with beach pebble-pattern tiles that match the flooring.*

A 12V pump-tap stainless-steel sink has been added in the base of the seat by the load door. A grey washing bowl and grey and pebble-pattern floor tiles laid in a check pattern harmonize with the original two-tone grey interior panels.

degreaser. The original Devon coolbox, fed by fresh air from the front grill, was beyond repair and has been replaced with a standard modern coolbox.

The Devon had originally been finished in Neptune Blue but Ant and Emma had had it resprayed in Savannah Beige paint (used in 1968) for a more subtle period look, and they wanted the interior fabrics to complement this. A period-style beige/cream/brown open check material sourced from VW Camper Curtains harmonizes perfectly with both the exterior colour and with the grey interior panels; VW Camper Curtains made up the curtains and tiebacks, and supplied extra material for the seats to be covered to match. The original Devon reversible style has been followed, and the seat

cushions are finished with grey vinyl on one side and matching fabric with a button finish on the rear. The cab seats were freshened up with fitted seat covers. The original plan had been to clean the heavily nicotine-stained headlining as it had no rips or tears, but it was too badly stained ever to come clean, despite many attempts, so they decided eventually to panel the roof in wood, as in early Westfalia campers, and matching wood panelling as on the units was used to keep the styling coherent.

Light grey floor tiles have been mixed with a pebble beach-pattern tile, and this has been carried through to the tabletop, which has been covered with the same pebble-pattern tiles. The addition of a remote MP3

RIGHT: Two 6 × 9 speakers and a sub-woofer have been sited under the rear seat.

BELOW: Reproduction seat covers in original style are a simple way to freshen up the cab seats, and the addition of Wolfsburg crest seat belts adds to the period look.

player, amp, head unit, two 6 × 9 speakers and a sub sited under the rear seat provides a modern sound system whilst travelling or simply relaxing.

Nearly all the materials used in the interior makeover came from a DIY superstore, and the finished result shows how a dramatic new look can be achieved on a budget, yet still be stylish and distinctive. The traditional look of the late 1960s Devon style has been retained, and this interior makeover has achieved everything the owners intended – period charm with a personal touch.

(Photographs courtesy of Ant Edensor)

RIGHT: Stainless-steel handles in a chilli pepper design add a contemporary and personal styling detail.

BELOW: The roof panelling blends well with new woodwork and original oak features such as the rear drawer unit.

period styling
1966 Microbus

The interior panels and seats have been finished in light grey and blue-grey vinyl to harmonize with the exterior colours; oak laminate flooring has been used to face the cabinet fronts and sides.

A striped canopy/sun awning fits above the open load doors to provide shade and air.

Starting from scratch to design a camping interior to suit an individual lifestyle enables owners to think carefully about exactly what facilities they really need, especially with regard to kitchen facilities. Most camping conversions from Devon *et al* always included cooking facilities (though early Westfalias had a camping stove as an optional extra rather than as standard equipment) – but for some families, small children and gas flames inside a bus don't mix,

and cooking in an awning means no lingering cooking smells clogging the interior. Will McLaughlin is one of those, and when designing the interior he decided against cooking in the van, and to carry gas and a cooker in dedicated storage areas instead. Part of the attraction of camping for Will and Kathleen is cooking in the open, especially barbecues, and by leaving a cooker unit out of the interior, more space has been made available for other things.

ABOVE: Plaid fabric for curtains and scatter cushions makes for a period feel, with red bringing in a touch of colour, whilst the grey and white coordinate with the interior colour scheme.

LEFT: The rear seat/rock-and-roll bed cushions are upholstered in blue-grey, with contrasting light grey centre sections to match the interior and door panels.

Having acquired a lovely 1966 Cumulus White/Sea Blue microbus from Arizona, Will sold on the microbus seats and set about looking at many different styles of period and original interiors before deciding on the layout and materials for his own camper. He wanted a period look, but function and usability were the key words: the interior was to be used by a family, and was not intended for sitting on show fields. After checking out 'complete' original interiors for sale, he soon decided that the amount of money needed to buy and refurbish one was not worth it, and that a better route would be to design and build his own, using the features and styling from 1960s interiors. This would enable him to combine some of the best features from the original versions he had seen, but to add some refinements of his own. As the bus was a bulkhead model, the classic Devon dinette layout was chosen, as this offered the best use of space for eating/relaxing/sleeping, with plenty of storage, and this was the starting point.

After fitting a metal-framed, Bluebird three-quarter rock-and-roll bed, Will bought two packs of oak laminate flooring from Floors 2 Go, and started

LEFT: Centre kick panels of the oak seat bases have been covered in blue-grey vinyl, whilst chrome air vents, socket covers and catches from IKEA bring in modern styling.

BELOW: The interior has a homely period feel, and has been designed to be functional and practical.

period styling: 1966 Microbus

RIGHT: A curtained wardrobe is sited in the rear, along with a grey vinyl-covered cabinet that contains electrical and hook-up fittings. Oak trim and chrome fittings keep the styling continuity.

ABOVE: The small rear cupboard has the trip switch for the mains hook-up, the 12V fuse box for the leisure battery supply, and the battery condition meter.

The wardrobe side and roof locker is covered in light grey vinyl with oak trim ends, and more chrome fittings are seen in additional 240V socket covers and twin spotlights.

A 12V pump tap and stainless-steel fridge have been mounted in a specially designed door unit, finished in oak and blue-grey vinyl to match, making excellent use of the dead space between the front door and front bench unit.

placing them in the van to work out how to get the look and function he was after. Despite being a designer he did not produce any drawings, but just started by fitting in the largest pieces of oak first and filling the gaps with MDF board covered in the same vinyl as the door cards and seat cushions. A hard-wearing lacquer finish was applied to the cabinets, and light grey and blue-grey vinyl from Martrim in Sandbach was chosen for a period feel and to coordinate with the exterior colours. Will then re-upholstered the seats and panels in two-tone vinyl, using the light grey vinyl for the roof cupboard and hanging space sides, and the blue-grey for the sink unit base. Vinyl-covered bench kick panels and chrome handles and catches from IKEA add a contemporary look. Matching detailing is continued with chrome-fronted 240V socket covers, spotlights and fridge vents, and grey vinyl flooring.

A flap-down table is fitted against the side wall between the bench seats, and when not in use is secured against the side of the van by a drop-down wooden stay. As the table leg is longer than the actual table, it has an adjustable foot end so that it folds cleanly under the table when in the travelling position. A top-accessed Waeco fridge has been built in under the front bench seat, and at the side of the rear seat is a pantry/storage with lift top that doubles as a shelf/worktop, with mains electric hook-up and a 12V leisure battery to power the fridge, two 12V reading spotlamps fitted at either side of the roof cupboard, and a Sony CD/DAB radio system. A box containing the trip switch for the mains hook-up, and the 12V fusebox for the leisure battery supply and the battery charger, is discretely mounted in the rear behind the curtained wardrobe. Additional green power comes from a window-mounted solar panel.

ABOVE: A Waeco top-loading fridge is sited under the front bench seat.

LEFT: An oak-faced cabinet at the side of the rear seat has top- and side-accessed storage areas, and the oak top doubles as a shelf/workspace.

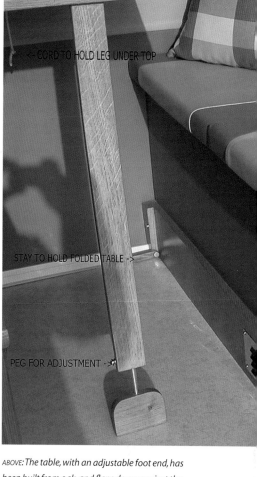

← CORD TO HOLD LEG UNDER TOP

STAY TO HOLD FOLDED TABLE →

PEG FOR ADJUSTMENT →

ABOVE: The table, with an adjustable foot end, has been built from oak, and flaps down against the side wall when not in use. The wooden stay to secure it whilst travelling can be seen at the end of the oak seat base panel.

BELOW: The addition of a padded steering wheel with Wolfsburg logo horn push, new fascias for the speedo and fuel gauge, and chromed ashtray, update the period look in the cab. The front kick panel and stereo head unit surround are also finished in matching blue-grey.

Clever use of the dead space by the front load door has been made by the design and fitting of a door-mounted sink unit, finished in oak and vinyl to match, with a 12V tap-actuated pump cold water supply and waste bottle; when the doors are closed the unit sits neatly at the seat end behind the bulkhead, and with the doors open, more floor/living space has been released and the sink is ready for use in the awning.

The cab has been kept clean and simple with matching vinyl seats and door and kick panels, but the addition of a padded Karmann Konnection steering wheel with Wolfsburg logo horn push, new fascias for the speedo and fuel gauge, and chromed ashtray, update the look. To finish the 1960s feel, a period Westy-style plaid fabric was sourced, and new curtains run up by Will's eighty-year-old mother: the muted red check brings a touch of contrasting colour to the interior, whilst the grey and white coordinate with, and tie in, the whole colour scheme.

Designing and building your own interior can be a comparatively inexpensive route to follow, and this lovely example shows how tasteful, classic styling can be updated, and retain its functional and period charm.

(Photographs courtesy of Will McLaughlin)

curvy comfort
1964 Split Camper

Flowing lines and curving cabinets by either door draw you into the interior.

ABOVE: Button-finish seat cushioning and warm oak wood make for an opulent feel. Armrests on both bench seats add to the luxurious living-room sofa look. Coordinating green and white check curtains, and carpeting that matches the seat fabric, make for a unified look.

BELOW: The curved rear side unit has drawers, with finger holes instead of protruding handles, to maximize use of the tall storage area. The top makes for a useful shelf, and hinges up to reveal more storage.

Bob and Angela Norfolk have been into classic cars for years, and used to have a Bay Viking conversion; however, they always hankered after a 'Splitty' for its cute looks and classic lines. So when a one-owner 1964 Canterbury Pitt came up for sale, they jumped at the chance. Finished in Pearl White, with a complete interior and pop-top roof, the bus also came with over forty years of documented history.

From the start, however, Bob and Angela decided to put their own mark on the bus and create something striking. Though the original interior was complete, they were not inspired by it, and they also preferred the clean line of

a fixed roof. Bob stripped out the interior and took the bus to Les of L. & R. Superbeetles, who carried out all the body and mechanical repairs. Initially Bob had the idea of replacing the pop top with a sunroof, but the lack of insulation, the noise, and the potential for leaks dissuaded him, and he ended up sourcing a complete donor roof for Les to fit! They opted for the classic two-tone look, and as green is a family favourite, chose Velvet Green under Pearl White in order to keep period authenticity. Deluxe chrome trim, six stainless-steel pop-outs, safari front windows and a side step add a mild custom touch.

ABOVE: *Like all the cabinet work, the large curved unit has no visible catches or hinges, to make for clean, unbroken flowing lines throughout the interior.*

LEFT: *The unit has a deep, circular, stainless-steel sink with pump tap, with storage for water containers under.*

With the bus nearly ready, thoughts turned to the interior. They knew they wanted something a bit funky and which retained a traditional look but had a modern edge, and therefore set about tramping show fields and reading magazines and books for ideas. They contacted Bernard Newbury, who suggested they also contact Simon Weitz of Interior Motive about having a bespoke interior built. Simon's work is known for its innovative and striking designs, coupled with quality craftsmanship. The initial brief was to design something with the soft, warm glow of wood and leather that harked back to the 1950s Pullman railway carriages, mixed in with the opulent and classy decor of the Orient Express.

Oak finish for all the cabinet work has been chosen for its warm honey colours, and Simon suggested that rather than sharp corners and angles, soft curves would create the flowing lines and the period feel they were after. Bob and Angela's experiences of camping with their Viking meant they had some clear ideas about what was needed or not needed in the interior: a dinette style of bench seating round a

table suited the bulkhead model layout perfectly, and there was no need for a built-in cooker unit (meaning no lingering fried bacon smells). The pullout bed had to have no intrusive handles showing, and Simon also suggested using push locks on the cupboard doors, which would mean unbroken smooth lines for the curving oak cabinet work.

A curved unit for the deep stainless-steel sink and pump tap, with water and waste bottles and storage for a porta potti under, is sited behind the bulkhead by the front load door, with the curve opening into the interior. Opposite this, in a style based upon the early Devons, is a matching unit that features curved front drawers to make

ABOVE: *The table flaps against the side wall when not in use. A curved extension slots on to the end for dining, and the chrome pedestal leg brings in a contemporary styling touch.*

BELOW: *Soft curves and clean lines are the hallmark of this interior design.*

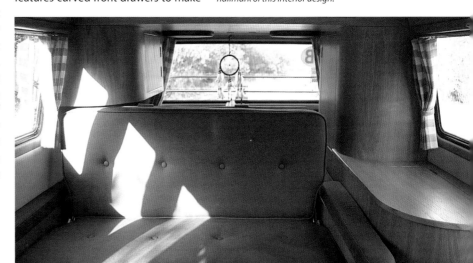

A motorized pop-up TV/DVD is discretely fitted in the bulkhead: it is completely hidden inside with a flush wooden top when not in use.

maximum use of space of the cabinet height, with more storage accessed via the hinged solid wood top that also provides a shelf/worktop area. The drawers are locked in place by the simple device of a metal rod that slides down from the top. The curving lines are followed through to the tall rear side cabinet, which has hanging space. Opposite this is a smaller cabinet, also curved to match the flowing lines; a closed roof unit, with speakers and spotlights in the base, runs between the two.

The rear seat is finished with curved front armrest sections, giving a luxury settee feel, both of which feature removable tops to reveal more storage. The facing bench seat is finished to match, and a flap-down table sits between the two. The table features a curved end, hinged extension, allowing it to store neatly against the sidewall, and a chrome single pedestal leg screws into the table base, so no floor well is needed. Behind the front bulkhead seat is another cabinet, with a shelf top, created by removing the spare wheel well; it has more storage, and also has a motorized 17in widescreen TV with Freeview wired to the stereo and SatNav to play DVDs. Bob had wanted a TV, but Angela did not want to see it dominating the interior,

ABOVE: Twin reading spots are hidden away in the roof locker base, which is where the speakers are also mounted. A flush door has a push lock catch, allowing them to drop down for use.
BELOW: The side door panels match the cab doors, keeping continuity of design.

ABOVE: The cab bench seat is trimmed in pale green leather with matching pleated green fabric insert sections to provide a coordinated design break between the cab and living areas.

so hiding it away here is a perfect solution: one touch on the remote and the TV glides smoothly up from its hiding place ready for use. Angela also requested lighting in the rear for reading, and Simon's solution is an ingenious touch-open door in the roof cabinet, which pops down to reveal twin eyeball spotlights.

With the interior taking shape, Bernard Newbury was called in to provide the finishing touches. He suggested mixing fabric and leather rather than having all leather upholstery, and also to have a design break to reverse the look between the cab and living areas. The cab seats have been trimmed in pale green leather with pleated dark green cloth insert panels, and to create a more relaxed feel in the rear, the rear seats are finished in the green cloth, with a button

finish that complements and contrasts with the cab finish and makes for a more homely feel. Interior panels have been trimmed to match, and matching green carpeting is fitted to cab and living areas.

The headliner is a beige-brown West of England cloth, which also covers the upper areas round the windows. The final touch is coordinating green and white check curtains, which hang from oak-finish open pelmet rails, with one set to screen the cab from the living area, a styling feature found on early Westfalias.

The finished interior combines period styling with modern design to create a striking, opulent and eminently practical interior, which maximizes the use of space. The unbroken curving lines open up the space and invite you inside to enjoy camping in comfort.

BELOW: The cab door panels are finished in pale green leather and have a pleated fabric centre section to match the side doors. Green carpet matching that in the living area is also used in the cab.

transporter transformer
1987 Autohomes Camper

This T3 shows how an unremarkable, almost bland family camper can be transformed into a mean gangster with a hidden heart. Taking its name and inspiration from a song by Goldfrapp, 'Black Cherry' is dark and hard on the outside, but warm and soft on the inside. Built in 1987, it came with factory-fitted extras such as a swivelling passenger seat, twin sunroofs and Black/Silver two-tone paintwork. It was converted to a camper by Autohomes

using the traditional layout of kitchen unit under the windows with fridge, stainless steel twin hob and sink, and storage, pull-out bed, porta potti seat, pedestal-leg table, wardrobe/storage in the rear and underslung water tanks.

Ian Farrar, founder of the Vanarchy Event, already had a T3 with a seriously fast engine, but wanted something more comfortable for camping. Having bought this, he then set about planning a totally new look. The outside would be

The original furniture and layout has been retained, as it blended in with Ian's plans.

ABOVE: Cerise leather has been used to upholster seats and cushions for a luxurious look and feel, which is also startling!

ABOVE: The cerise and black colour scheme is continued in the cab with cerise pinstriping detail on the cab doors, matching overlocked footmat edges, and cerise leather gear-lever sleeve.

LEFT: The rear seat has been upholstered using a pleated pattern with roll-edge front.

black (with tinted windows adding to that hard gangster look), but the inside would upturn all expectations and be finished in soft cerise. The interior cabinets were all still very clean, and the 1980s grey-white grain melamine finish would blend well with Ian's plans, so he decided to work around them.

The bus was fitted with a German body-style kit and bumpers, and then painted in VW Black Magic metallic paint (LC 9Z). Next on the agenda for that mean look was a serious lowering job, 18in DGT0019 alloy wheels, some clear light lenses and tinted windows.

The bus was then taken to Anderson and Ryan in Coventry for trimming. Formerly trimmers for Jaguar, their clients now range from Rolls-Royce to Puff

ABOVE: Contrasting detail for the seats is provided by black piping.

BELOW: A swivelling front seat adds space and flexibility. The whole interior is fully carpeted in soft grey carpet.

The dashboard top has been finished with matching grey carpet.

Daddy, so Ian's plans were no shock to them! In fact they suggested subtle finishing touches, and sourced the co-ordinating curtain fabric. Taking up the black cherry theme, the seats have all been finished in soft cerise leather with black piping, and all the panels in deep grey leather with a cerise pin-striping motif. Soft grey carpet is fitted throughout and on the porta potti seat

base, which is topped with a matching cerise leather cushion.

Finishing details include grey foot mats edged with cerise overlocking, cerise grab handles, and even a cerise leather casing for the gear stick. The luxurious feel is continued with soft, dark grey velour for the headlining, and the grey curtain fabric has cerise needle-striping to match. The addition of a full-

ABOVE: *Attention to detail can be seen in the cerise grab handles and grey curtains with a cerise pinstripe.*

LEFT: *The roof is lined in dark grey velour, adding to the luxurious look.*

LEFT: A cerise all-weather mat is perfect for standing outside on wet grass.

BELOW: The original units run under the windows, following the traditional layout, and contain the cooker, sink and fridge.

on Sony CD system with demountable speakers means that music can be blasted outside the bus when sitting outside relaxing at a show, whilst a cherry-smelling air freshener is a nice finishing touch when you enter the inside.

The contrast between the 'sinister care home look' (Ian's own words) and soft voluptuous interior, coupled with the looks on people's faces when the sliding door is opened, is exactly what Ian wanted when he set out to create a bus that would startle, yet still be functional. This is one mean gangster with a soft heart.

LEFT: The hanging closet is also accessible from the rear.
BELOW: The removable buddy seat/porta potti unit has been finished to match.

13

Vantasia
1970 Dormobile

When Peter Pimley took his tired 1970 Dormobile to Paul Smith for an interior makeover, his brief to Paul was simple: 'I want something here by the door with a sink in it, and a seat that curves from behind that bit of the front bulkhead and comes round to meet it.' In the previous four years of ownership Peter had sorted the mechanics and body, including a repaint in a striking modern metallic red, and decided that the hacked about/rebuilt Dormie interior needed updating with something a bit more modern and classy, in keeping with its outside appearance. Paul, a woodworker by trade, and Diane Finch, an upholsterer who used to work trimming Morgan sports cars, had just set up in business as Vantasia, and this was their first project. The open brief allowed Paul and Diane freedom to add their own creative design touches, some of which were talked through with Peter, and some of which they just went ahead and did! They likened the process to the television programme *Changing Rooms*, with Peter eventually being called in to see the finished bus!

The first job was to get the cabinet and seating to work. Using polished oak frames and oak veneer for a traditional look, Paul set about designing and building a curving corner seat that would maximize space but also create

ABOVE: The curving rear corner seat maximizes the floor area, making for a spacious feel to the interior.

RIGHT: The deep burgundy upholstery with white piping – chosen to complement the exterior paintwork, coupled with light oak cabinets and flooring – makes for a classy, modern interior. Finishing details, such as the matching burgundy curtains with white ties, carry through the colour theme.

ABOVE: *Cab seats, upholstered in matching burgundy vinyl, have a stitched VW logo on the headrests, and the white racing stripe design and white piped edges carry through the finishing detail of the rear seat.*

ABOVE: *The stainless-steel sink, set into a light Formica top that matches the television unit shelf, has an electric pump tap and a modern smoked glass lid. The spare wheel, kept in the rear, has a matching red/white vinyl cover.*

LEFT: *Every possible storage area has been exploited, as here behind the seats.*

unbroken lines – not an easy task. The seating also had to be able to convert to a bed and have storage under. Peter had already decided that a table and a cooker could be dispensed with, as he did not like the idea of a gas flame in the confined interior space, or the grease and smells from cooking inside.

Cooking is done outside under an awning using a two-burner hob that stows neatly in the cupboard under the sink unit. The stainless-steel sink is surrounded by a pale Formica worktop, and the lid is the smoked heat-resistant glass variety often used for motorhome or caravan cooker lids. The use of

modern materials like this creates a very contemporary-looking design.

Peter then thought it would be good to be able to watch television in bed, so Paul decided that the best way to meet this request was to design and build a specific matching unit sited against the bulkhead behind the passenger seat. A

The long seat under the windows is upholstered in pleated burgundy vinyl, with white piping for contrast; the seat curves round to meet a cabinet with fitted sink unit.

LEFT: A 12V television stands on the Formica shelf top of the oak unit behind the passenger seat for viewing. Gold handles on the cabinets add a touch of luxury.

BELOW: The cabinet has been specially built round the dimensions of the television, which is stored in the top section of the unit when not in use.

BELOW: For cooking in the awning, a free-standing twin-hob burner is carried under the sink unit.

12V television, sourced from a marine specialist, sits snugly in the cabinet and can also be sited on the shelf, topped with matching Formica, for better viewing. Gold handles add a touch of luxury.

With the new, original-style headliner in place, all the struts for the elevating roof were refurbished and painted in red and white, pelmets with spotlights mounted above the side windows, and a small open-fronted

Spotlights are mounted on to an oak pelmet.

storage unit fitted in the roof at the rear. Additional storage is sited behind the rear seat section, and in the luggage area above the engine (where spare bed cushions are also carried). The final job was the fitting of hard-wearing oak laminate flooring, which brings the interior together by creating light and harmonizing with the surrounding cabinet work.

The bus had already been painted in Diablo Red (from the Peugeot metallics range) under Old English White, and Diane chose a harmonizing burgundy vinyl for the upholstery. The seat cushions had to be carefully shaped before adding stitching and cream piping for contrast. Two of Diane's other personal touches can be seen on the cab seats: a racing stripe (in matching cream) pays

ABOVE: *Oak laminate flooring extends into the gangway area and matches the light oak woodwork. The seat back panels are also faced with oak.*

RIGHT: *Seat cushions have been carefully shaped to follow the curved lines of the seating.*

homage to her sports car background, and the addition of a VW logo embroidered on to each headrest. (The cab seats, incidentally, came from a Rover Metro and look unrecognizable here!) Matching burgundy curtains with white ties, and spotlights mounted on oak pelmets finish the overall look.

The whole project took a couple of months from conception to realization, although there are still things such as the elevating roof that are a 'work in progress'!

Vantasia have worked from a simple starting brief to create a very stylish, hand-built interior that works well both aesthetically and practically, and which has been designed completely around the way in which the customer wants to use his bus. The flowing lines of the curved seating call out to be lounged on, and Peter can now sit and watch the world through his windows or on his television, and take time to enjoy 'chilling' in comfort in the company of friends.

ABOVE: *Additional storage is built in under the seating.*

BELOW: *A roomy bed is made up by laying down specially shaped cushions on to boards.*

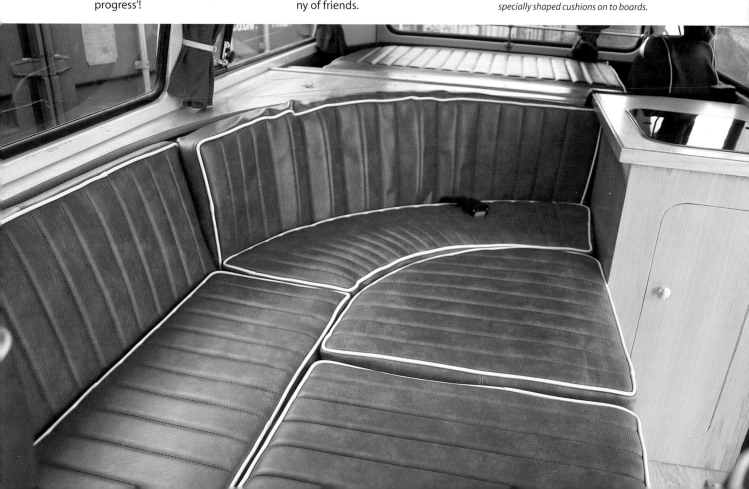

custard and calypso
1971 Bay Window Camper

When Steve Williams took his 1971 Bay, called 'Custard', to John and Sue at Calypso Campers for an interior refit, his starting point was simply lots of storage and enough floor space for a travel cot. The bus had already been repainted in Opal Lifestyle Purple under Yellow Gel, and he quite liked the existing pastel blue and yellow check curtains and scatter cushions, and wanted interior colours that would harmonize with these. Calypso's interior conversions are all one-off, bespoke designs tailored to the individual owner's needs, and they also do everything in house, such as sourcing cookers and fittings. John sat down in the bus with Steve and sketched out various possibilities that would suit his requirements, and having decided the interior layout, they then looked through colour samples for the furniture finish and trim.

To maximize space, Steve had decided a cooker was not on his list of requirements; being a fixed roof camper he felt cooking in the awning was more practical, and the emphasis was to be on storage. John planned out a side unit, three-quarter rock-and-roll bed, a single seat (both with storage under), and a side two-door wardrobe with roof locker to meet the space and storage requirements: this has worked out to be both practical and ergonomic. Having access to the wardrobe from

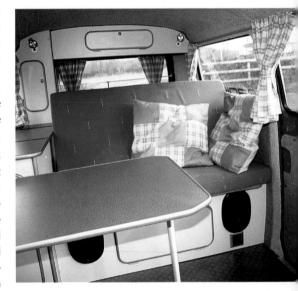

ABOVE: The interior reflects modern styling trends in materials and looks, to give a contemporary light, airy feel.

LEFT: The interior has been finished in blue and grey to harmonize with the existing pastel blue and yellow check curtains and scatter cushions.

LEFT: *Cabinets have been finished in 'Graffiti Grey' with silver trim edging and door surrounds and chrome push handles. The wardrobe can be accessed from the front and side, and twin chrome spotlights create ambient lighting.*
BELOW: *The side unit has ample storage with a side door and lift-up shelf top.*

both the side and rear is a particularly good design idea, and the access to side storage via a hinged top door or the front-facing section also maximizes flexibility of use.

The blue and grey interior is practical and modern in styling and look. The door and side panels have been lined in Azure Blue, and the roof and sides above the windows with Silver Trimliner, which harmonizes perfectly with the Graffiti Grey units finished with silver trim edging and door surrounds. All the cabinet work is made from German 'Vohringer Ply', a top quality, hardwearing material that is a trademark of Calypso interiors, and the table and worktops are finished with heat-resistant 'Puntinella', the slightly darker, silver-grey finish, again keeping the colour theme consistent. The bed and seat cushions have been upholstered in Teardrop Blue, which is flecked with silver-grey detailing, and brings a bit of

...lue upholstery has a silver fleck pattern to harmonize with the interior colours.

LEFT: *A single seat maximizes floor space and has additional storage and power management system in the base.*

65

ABOVE: *The colour coordination is carried through with mid-grey, check plate-pattern vinyl flooring and azure blue interior panels topped with silver trimliner, which is also used as headliner. Floor space has been maximized to allow for a travel cot to sit inside. Speakers and 240V sockets have been fitted in the seat bases.*

LEFT: *The corners of units are rounded for safety, and the side unit is topped with dark grey Puntinella to contrast with the lighter grey of the units.*

additional colour to lift the interior. The single, folding-leg side table has a slide action, making for ease of access around it, and the flooring has been finished with a mid-grey check plate pattern vinyl for a wipe-clean hardwearing floor with a hint of industrial design heritage. Twin spots and two roof strip-lights create ambient lighting, and 240V/12V sockets allow a variety of appliances to run from the leisure battery or hook-up.

Steve had already fitted Porsche Recaro front seats, and these have been re-covered in 'Evolve' – a grey, high quality leather-finish vinyl for that luxurious look as well as comfortable travelling. Yellow piping and stitched centre panel inserts in a paler grey add a sporty, racing look, and an Empi shifter, custom pedals, Wolfsburg Edition chrome window-winder handles, chrome bud vase and chrome fire extinguisher all add custom finishing detailing in the cab.

The interior is light, spacious and airy, and represents an excellent compromise between practicality, cost and space: the large floor area is available as a result of having just one single seat,

The slide-action table has a single folding leg and is topped in dark grey, heat-resistant Puntinella to match the side unit.

ABOVE: An Empi shifter, custom alloy pedals, chrome bud vase and fire extinguisher and Mooneyes badging all add custom-finishing detailing in the cab.

LEFT: Porsche Recaro front seats have been re-covered in a grey leather-finish vinyl with yellow piping and stitched centre panel inserts in a paler grey to add a sporty, racing look.

and this suits their needs for a travel cot perfectly. Things move on, however, and Steve is currently toying with the idea of having a single unit fitted behind the passenger seat, possibly to fit a television/DVD unit. Adding some-

thing like this at a later stage is very easy to do, and it would be made to match the rest of the cabinet work. He would also quite like to have the bench and single seat reupholstered to match the cab seats.

RIGHT: Chrome Wolfsburg window winders add a custom styling influence.

BELOW: Cab door and kick panels and under-seat flooring have also been trimmed in Azure Blue.

circle time
1964 Split Camper

LEFT: This distinctive circular-style interior was inspired by seating at a nightclub, and has been assembled from a kit using birch marine-grade ply.

BELOW: Burgundy Red vinyl, with white piping and detailing, makes for a distinctive look that harmonizes with the exterior colours of the bus.

This interior, with circular-style seating, took its inspiration from a local club where owners Simon Fitzjohn and Ruth Knowles used to enjoy relaxing with friends. They had acquired a sorry-looking 1964 'Splitty', totally bare and in need of full restoration, and having finished the mechanics and body, talk turned to the interior. They checked out many magazines, books and actual bus interiors at shows, with the aim being to create something different and eye-catching, but also functional. For them, relaxing with friends is an essential part of their lifestyle, and the interior had to reflect this. They wanted more seating and fewer cabinets, since 'chilling' inside the bus was more important than cooking in it! The normal square seating just did not create the same vibe – but then they remembered this style of circular seating from a local club, and having fitted a sunroof, what could be better than sitting round with friends under open skies...?

Originally they were going to build the seating themselves, but then they found a company that actually produced the circular style of seating they wanted, at a price within their budget. The layout had the added bonus of under-seat storage, and the seating

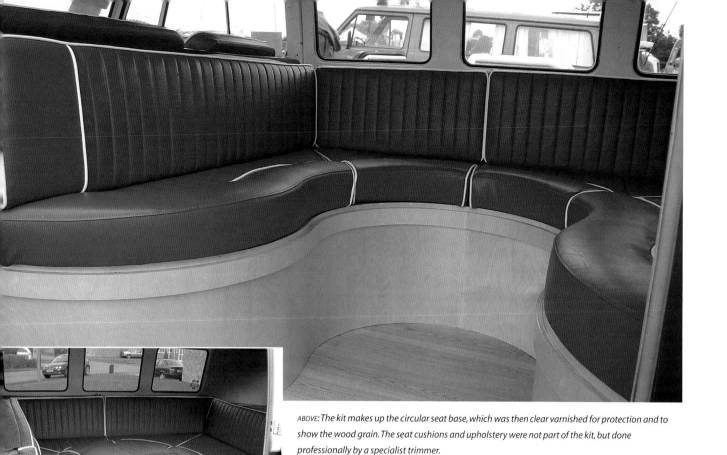

ABOVE: *The kit makes up the circular seat base, which was then clear varnished for protection and to show the wood grain. The seat cushions and upholstery were not part of the kit, but done professionally by a specialist trimmer.*

ABOVE: *The bed is made up by laying specially shaped cushions onto boards.*

BELOW: *Cab and load door panels are finished in matching red and white vinyl, with horizontally pleated centre sections for contrast.*

could also be laid out as a bed – somewhere cosy to retire to when friends stumbled back to their own campers! The kit was supplied by www.busfurniture.co.uk (now sadly defunct) and the units came all ready assembled, not flat packed, with the cabinets finished in a light-coloured birch marine grade-based ply. To keep costs down Simon chose the unvarnished option, and in order to keep the grain and colour of wood on show, and to protect it, applied a clear varnish himself before fitting it into the bus.

The fitting itself was quite straightforward, and Simon and Ruth are very pleased with the build quality. Using a kit like this is ideal for someone lacking cabinet-making skills or time, and has the added attraction of being a cheaper alternative to a one-off design! Laminate wood flooring harmonizes with the seat bases, and is hard-wearing and easy to keep clean.

They had chosen Metallic NightFire Red under Off White for the exterior colours, with the interior metal finished in the same colours, and this provided

ABOVE: *The original rear drawers have been retained, and the three additional cushions used for making the bed are stored above them.*

RIGHT: *The VW logo and bus name, embroidered in white, add personal styling touches.*

The seat cushions have been made up in separate sections for practical ease of use. Smooth rolled edges, pleated seat base sections and seat backs, and white piping create a classy look as well as being comfortable.

the theme for the interior colour scheme. Initially they had wanted a predominantly white interior with white vinyl upholstery, but soon realized that white would show marks easily, and that a red would be more practical. So Burgundy Red was chosen as the main colour and used throughout, with white detailing for contrast. The cab seats have white piping and white inset-stitched panels, whilst the lounge seat has smooth sitting edges with stitching details and white piping along all cushion edges and between the stitched/plain area on the base cushions. The door cards are patterned in plain red and stitched white to match.

Ifor Evans, of Evans Upholstery in Peterborough, carried out all the trimming, and was most helpful with suggestions to improve the practicality of the interior, for example having wood bases to the seat cushions to make access to under-storage easier, securing the cushions in place with pop studs, and using several cushions to form the seat, rather than just one!

Another part of Simon and Ruth's initial plan had been to incorporate the VW logo and the camper's name, Betsy, on the cab door cards, but it looked unbalanced when drawn out, so instead they decided to make use of the area above the engine bay. The

original drawers that sit in that area were still with the bus, and they decided to keep them and simply cleaned them up and waxed them. They then had the bus's name and a VW logo stitched in white into the cushion that sits above the drawers, with white piping breaking up the smooth area into panels. (This cushion and the two semi-circular ones also stored in the rear are used when making up the bed.) The use of contrasting detail is continued in touches such as the white interior door handles and dash grab handle, and the white steering wheel with white horn bush and red horn ring.

The end result is a distinctive and stylish interior that suits their needs and lifestyle. Using a kit has given them the interior look and seating plan they wanted at a competitive price, and has also allowed them to add their own individual touches in choice of colours and finish for the wood and upholstery. In use, the interior has done exactly the job they intended, with the bonus of having that 'wow' factor they were after. Future plans include fitting a sound system and possibly a television/DVD – but until then they are content just to sit around with friends and put the world to rights.

The red/white colour theme extends into the cab area with finishing details such as the burgundy carpet, and white door and grab handles, white steering wheel and column, and red horn ring, all of which are colour coded with the exterior paintwork.

The cab seats are trimmed in matching red vinyl with pleated white insert panels to coordinate with the door panels.

classical bling
1962 High Roof

ABOVE: A large double-door roof unit is sited at the rear, with speakers with louvre outlets at either side.

LEFT: The cab retains a stock look with the subtle addition of gauges and CB radio. The blue/ white theme is carried through on the interior panels and white door and grab handles.

The special body *Hochdach* (High Roof) factory model was introduced in 1961, and quickly found favour with businesses wanting to take full advantage of the increased roof space and standing room inside. Very few of these models still survive, but as can be seen here, they offer an ideal base for a roomy camping conversion.

Owner Simon Coldwell acquired the bus as a Swedish import in a fairly rough condition, with some added (and poorly fitted) side windows. He is a long-time fan of the look of commercial vehicles, and being 6ft 6in (2m) tall, the Hi-Roof model was perfect for him as it meant he could actually stand up inside! After the usual body repairs, he had new upper side panels specially fabricated by Creative Engineering, before having the bus repainted in the classic commercial colour of Dove Blue. A full-length roofrack and ladder (both of which had to be tailor-made to fit)

have been added to give that period 'working' look. Polished Safaris front screens, an opening rear window and an ally side-step add a bit of 'bling', and the addition of Deluxe chrome belt-line trim gives a mild custom look, as well as complementing and breaking up the large expanses of blue paintwork. US-spec bumpers, finished in white, add to the overall styling, and the front badge and wheels are also painted in white to contrast with the Dove Blue.

LEFT: The rear hatch panels have been trimmed to match.

BELOW: The carpeted rear area has Devon-style twin-drawers, flanked by large storage cupboards on either side.

As a commercial vehicle it was completely empty inside, which gave Simon the chance to design an interior that would suit his needs. He wanted something finished in wood that had a classic, period feel and which would allow him to sleep and relax in comfort. A built-in cooker, sink and fridge were considered non-essential items for Simon's needs, and as he did not want to cook in the van, the rear seat could run the full width. Taking inspiration from the 1960s Devon layouts, he decided that a dinette style of seating, where a bed could be made up by putting the table flat between the bench seats, would work well and keep a period feel.

Having seen work by Vaughn and Tim of Custom, Classic and Retro Interiors featured in magazines, he liked the Devon-influenced styling of their work, and commissioned them to build an interior to his basic design brief. The cabinets have been hand-built from oak, and to keep that 1960s Devon feel, the door fronts are finished in gloss black laminate over birch ply. Curved, D-shaped, stainless-steel cupboard handles add a contemporary look to the classic design. A large, two-door storage unit has been built across the

BELOW: A folding magazine rack is another Devon styling touch. Colour coordinated scatter cushions add to the overall look.

ABOVE: Devon influences can be seen in the way the bed base is made up using the folding magazine rack and table top. Note the handy location of the church key on the seat end.

BELOW: Bedding has been carefully chosen to coordinate with the colour scheme.

The seat cushions are laid on the base to make a roomy, comfortable double bed.

rear roof section, flanked by speakers with louvre grills cut out in the wood. Under this is a drop-down television monitor that is also hooked to a Playstation 2 to provide entertainment. The rear area has storage cupboards on either side, and additional storage is provided by the twin drawer unit over the engine compartment, another Devon influence.

The table has a very modern feel, with a matching gloss black laminate top and single chrome pedestal leg, and in keeping with the Devon theme,

the bed is made up simply by laying the table down between the seats and rearranging the cushions. A magazine rack mounted on the sidewall between the seats, as found on early Devons, also folds down to form part of the bed base.

A custom headlining in white vinyl has been fitted, which had to be made from scratch, including the bows, because panel vans had unlined roofs. Likewise interior side panels were specially made to measure. The seats, door and side panels have been upholstered

RIGHT: Black laminate-faced door fronts hark back to 1960s Devon interiors, and the addition of stainless-steel D-handles adds a modern styling touch. A drop-down television/ PlayStation monitor, sited under the roof lockers, provides entertainment.

ABOVE: The seats are finished in pleated navy vinyl with contrasting white piped edges. The coordinating Beetle-style bolsters cleverly reverse this colour scheme.

BELOW: Interior and door panels have been finished in navy vinyl with pleated detail white centre sections, which complements the pleated navy seat cushions.

in navy blue vinyl to harmonize with the classic Dove Blue exterior, and cream vinyl has been used on the cab kick panel and centre sections of door and side panels to complement the white exterior detailing of the front badge, wheels and bumpers.

The seat cushions have been box pleated, as have the padded cream insert sections of the panels, which breaks up plain surfaces, and the seat cushions in both cab and living areas have been finished with cream piping to create a unified look. A pair of Beetle-style bolsters, in reverse colour scheme of cream with navy piping, and scatter cushions in blue/cream/grey open check, provide the finishing touches for a modern stylish interior that still retains a period look. The retro-modern feel is further enhanced by pre-metric-size black and white floor tiles laid in the traditional check pattern.

(Photographs courtesy of Simon Coldwell)

BELOW: The floor-mounted table is topped with black gloss laminate to match the door fronts, and black and white floor tiles laid in a traditional check pattern keep the classic period theme.

retro modern
1998 LWB T4 Panel Van

ABOVE: Plenty of storage/hanging space is provided in the rear cabinets and a small bedside locker.

RIGHT: The interior has been hand-built from solid pine, with a matching pine-panelled roof, to give a warm, period look.

This 1998 LWB T4 started life as a builder's van before Mike Williams spotted it for sale with Totally T4. They had repainted it in VW Metallic Diving Blue and added smart Totally T4 graphics, and Mike immediately saw the potential to create a distinctive exterior look coupled with a cosy camping interior. Being an LWB model meant there was more room and space to work with, and from the outset Mike wanted some-

thing stylish and practical that would make a striking impression on the local North Devon beaches. The addition of a cab sunroof and T5-type side windows from Vansport let in much needed light, as well as transforming the panel van appearance; other exterior styling touches come from Audi A8 wheels with VW centre caps, colour-coded bumpers and mirrors, and blacked-out VW badges. A 60mm lowering job adds

to the custom look, and the clean exterior lines have been maintained by using a compressor fridge (no vent grills) and water tank that is filled from inside. A clever touch is the fitting of mains hook-up in the nearside fog light, which is a dummy light – the light is simply removed and the hook-up pulled out to connect.

With no interior at all in the van, Mike and Nikki were able to work completely

LEFT: *The stylish interior could easily grace the glossy pages of any up-market conversion brochure.*

BELOW: *The Smev hob, grill and sink unit provide up-to-the-minute fittings as used on expensive motor caravans.*

ABOVE: *The pine interior recreates a classic Scandinavian kitchen look. The fridge door has been faced to blend in with the cabinets.*

BELOW: *Hard-wearing laminate flooring has a hint of blue in the shading to echo the outside colour and the seat fabric.*

to their own ideas. Inspiration came from those wooden beach huts found around the coast, and all the cabinets have been built from solid pine and pine panelling – no veneers here! A good friend, Dan, built the interior to their design, and the classic layout of kitchen and storage running under the side windows opposite the load door was chosen as the most space effective; they also decided to dispense with a table, as they prefer to sit outside to eat.

Behind the driver is the kitchen area, with compressor fridge, modern glass-

ABOVE: *Montana Blue fabric has been used to upholster the cab seats and rear seat/bed cushions.*

BELOW: *The quality of the craftsmanship can be seen in curved worktop sections and pine-clad window surrounds.*

The cab is basically as it left the factory, and still feels modern in styling.

fronted Smev grill and storage cupboards, and on top of this, set into a solid pine worktop, is the stylish, smoked-glass topped, stainless-steel Smev sink with electric pump tap and twin hob. The storage units behind this are inset back from these to create more space for the rear seat/bed. This runs to meet a full height section in the rear with twin storage areas/hanging

space and a battery condition meter. A roof locker, with inset spotlights, sits at the very rear.

The tailgate lifts to reveal a two-door boxed storage area under the rear section of the bed base, and push-button flush-locking latches have been fitted to all cupboard doors.

The seat cushions have been upholstered in a hard-wearing Montana Blue

fabric to coordinate with the exterior colour, all the interior walls have been lined with grey interior carpet, and the whole of the roof from the cab area to the rear has been panelled in matching pine, recreating that early Westfalia camper look. The natural wood theme is continued with hard-wearing laminate

BELOW: Additional storage is provided by a twin-door locker situated under the bed cushion at the rear.

ABOVE: Grey-carpeted walls and coordinating grey/white-striped curtains keep the interior styling subtle and understated.

BELOW: The bed width has been increased by setting the worktop/locker and rear cabinets slightly back from the main kitchen section.

flooring with a hint of blue in the pattern, which is perfect for sweeping sand away or wiping clean with no effort. Ambient lighting is provided by tungsten strip lights mounted above the windows.

The addition of two swivelling captain's seats in the cab, upholstered to match the rear seat, makes for a spacious and roomy living area that takes full advantage of the extra length of the LWB model. A 125 amp leisure battery, twin 240V sockets and 9 × 5 speakers (fed by a Pioneer head unit in the cab) are discreetly sited under the seat, and extra security for valuables is catered for by a safe, which has also been tucked away here.

Many factory T4 and T5 conversions have an inevitable sameness about them, but this T4 has achieved something different. The exterior is distinctive, with a nod towards custom styling; and while the interior has all the specs of a modern factory-fitted camper, the use of natural pine blends contemporary and modern styling to give a homely, warm feel – unlike the cold, almost clinical, neutral laminates favoured by many modern conversions. The layout is spacious and roomy, and its well thought-out practicality can be seen in touches such as the fact that all the storage cupboards can be easily accessed without moving the seat or cushions. **(Photographs courtesy of Mike Wood)**

BELOW: A closed roof locker provides more storage, and twin spots have been mounted in the base for reading.

converting a caravette
1970 Devon Caravette

The original Devon roof with two-door roof locker and handles has been kept to preserve some of the van's heritage.

Creating an individual interior need not cost the earth, or have to involve the services of a professional interior conversion company; nor does it need finely honed building and woodworking skills. The interior of this 1970 low light Bay may have been built on a budget by owner Andy Holder, but in no way is it a cheap and cheerful basic job, and Andy also has the satisfaction of having designed and created it all himself.

The bus was originally a Devon Caravette conversion, but by the time Andy acquired it, very little was left of the original Devon craftsmanship, apart from the bed, rear drawers and twin door roof locker. The single seats and most cabinets had been ripped out and replaced with some poorly made cabinets, and all the original red door cards and side panels and woodwork had been painted over with streaky white emulsion.

The rear seat base and new side unit have been faced with beech laminate for a contemporary look.

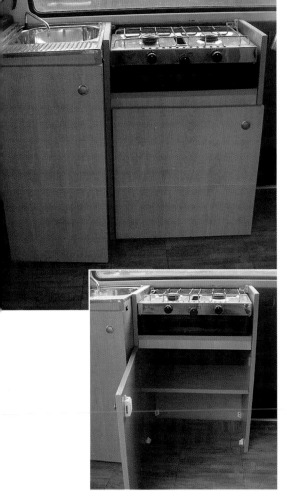

BELOW: A new kitchen unit for the sink and cooker has been built to sit behind the driver's seat. Chrome push-button handles work well with the light colour of the beech laminate.

ABOVE: The kitchen unit is in two sections, with the cooker cupboard set back to maximize floor space.

ABOVE: Shelving in the cooker section maximizes storage space.

BELOW: The side unit has an electric fridge with storage under the shelf top.

With so much missing, Andy decided it was pointless even to contemplate trying to restore the interior to its original layout, but he wanted to retain features such as the original door cards, bed and roof locker, and add to them sympathetically to give a modern stance to a period feel. Having previously owned a late 1970s Devon Moonraker he had a good idea of what worked and was useful (or what did not), and as the bus was to be a camper and not a day van, he wanted both washing and cooking facilities.

A fridge was also to be included, but as he did not want to cut the body for vents, it would have to be a version that could run off a leisure battery/mains hook-up system only. Because Andy was not starting from scratch with an empty van, the design had to work around the features he wanted to retain, so he opted to site the fridge at the end of the bed by the load door (as in the original Caravette

ABOVE: Modern fabric in red/white check for curtains and cushions brings colour and modern styling into the interior.

design), and to have the kitchen area in a unit behind the driver's seat. He also wanted to retain a clean front on the bus, meaning the spare wheel would have to stay inside at the rear.

The first job was to clean all the grim white emulsion from the panels and door cards – a job that took hours of elbow grease and copious amounts of detergent! With the red panels starting to look good, he then searched for wood and fabrics that would harmonize and give that contemporary look. For wood he chose beech laminate sheets, sourced from a local wood company, and set about building the cabinet for the cooker and sink unit.

The sink section, with electric pump tap, is offset behind the driver, with the cooker cabinet set back slightly to give more floor space. The design evolved during the build – for example, the internal shelves were not part of the original plan, but were well worth the extra work. The stainless-steel sink with electric pump tap and two-burner hob/grill were sourced from eBay, and the basic 12V/240V fridge from an online camping store. Push-button chrome handles and catches, supplied by Just Kampers, have been fitted to the cabinets to match the modern styling of the beech laminate.

The bed unit has been sanded back and lightly varnished, keeping the original Devon drawers and above-engine unit that can also be accessed via the rear seat back; the roof locker was similarly renovated. Wood block-pattern vinyl bathroom floor tiles that coordi-

ABOVE: A removable flat-screen television/DVD, kept in a fabric carry case, clips on the bulkhead behind the passenger seat. The red interior panels have been cleaned up, thus retaining another original period feature.

RIGHT: The Laura Ashley red/white open check fabric coordinates with the original red interior panels, and the pale green relief echoes the exterior Mango Green paintwork.

ABOVE: The original Devon rear drawer unit and bed base have also been kept intact. The spare wheel with matching fabric cover is kept in the rear so that the classic look of the front is not spoiled.

RIGHT: The flooring is wood block-pattern vinyl tiles, easy to lay and maintain.

nate with the beech cabinet work have been laid on the floor. The electric hook-up and socket has been mounted to the belly pan underneath the bus, freeing up valuable cupboard space inside. As well as providing power for the fridge, it also feeds a removable TFT television with built-in Freeview and DVD player, mounted directly behind the passenger seat using a fabric television case.

The finishing touch is the use of a modern plaid fabric for the seat cushions and curtains that brings the interior styling together and adds some colour. A 10m roll of Laura Ashley fabric was bought via the internet, and Andy's mum, Linda, made up seat cushion covers and curtains. The bold red/white open check pattern coordinates well with the red interior panels, whilst the green relief stripes echo the Mango Green exterior paintwork.

Like any personal project, the interior is still a 'work in progress', and Andy has ideas for further refinements, for example building a single buddy seat and adding spotlights in the rear. The use of beech laminate wood and a modern fabric have created the contemporary styling Andy wanted, and the interior is spacious and airy, with the new units blending perfectly with the original pieces. The fact that it has not cost thousands to create this individual look is an added bonus!

(Photographs courtesy of Andy Holder)

LEFT: A wooden snail mascot sits on the dash as a reminder that slow and steady still gets there in the end!

BELOW: The red interior panels had all been emulsioned over in white, but have been carefully cleaned so that this original feature could be retained.

all mod cons
1985 Panel Van

Using a panel van as the base for creating a camping interior offers a perfect blank canvas from which to start; however, whilst there is no interior to remove, and the lack of panels and headlining makes for easy laying down of wiring or cables, windows usually need to be cut in. Sitting in a totally empty space deciding how to fill it can be both daunting and inspiring!

This 1985 panel van started life as a Norwegian Army bus. Painted metallic green, and given two tinted side windows, Porsche Cup alloys and a Momo steering wheel, transformed it into a striking custom conversion – but the owner, Neil Dyke, was at a loss as to how to proceed with the interior, so called in Jon and Sue at Calypso Campers to create something a bit different for him. He had a set budget, and the only things on his wish list were a bed, a television and mains hook-up – and maybe a microwave! He had notions of unsubtle, green-striped interior panels, but after discussions with them, decided to leave the interior completely in their safe hands, knowing that what they came up with would incorporate his wants in a stylish and striking way.

Having carried out over 170 interior conversions, each one unique and

BELOW: The classic clean lines and neutral, calm greys are emphasized by the bold use of bright green piping and centre sections on the seating.

BELOW: The interior has been finished in coordinating greys, with a grey slate tile-effect vinyl flooring, for a contemporary look. The cabinets are angled cleanly round to the bulkhead, maximizing space.

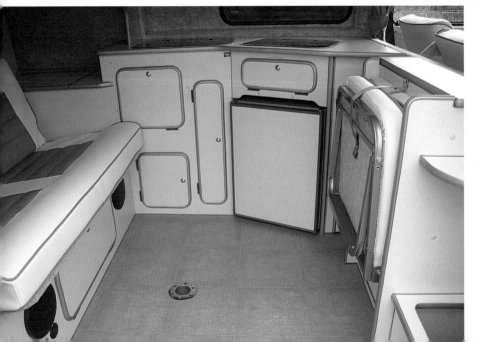

ABOVE: The circular table, finished to match the cabinet work, maximizes space and makes for easy access to kitchen units. The chrome pedestal leg adds to the modern feel of the interior.

ABOVE: A motorized TV screen is installed behind the buddy seat.

BELOW: The single folding bulkhead seat has been widened to make it more comfortable.

ABOVE: Cab seats are trimmed in Light Grey and Eden Green to match the rear seats.

purpose-built, Jon was now faced with the task of coming up with something new! With virtually a free hand and a generous budget, he took his initial inspiration from the tatty chipboard L-shaped unit that ran across part of the side wall and half of the bulkhead: from this he designed a larger kitchen unit to run in a similar position, only angled to create more worktop space.

The unit contains a large fridge, with additional shelved storage cupboards and a drawer; set into the top is a stainless-steel Smev two-burner hob, and a separate sink/tap featuring a modern smoked glass work surface. Running to meet this is a lower storage unit/table

top area with a two-door (side and rear) shelved wardrobe in the rear, and a roof cupboard with twin spotlights. Sited above the lower part of the side unit is equipment normally found in expensive motorhomes – a microwave, below which is more storage, shelving and a circular downlighter operated by touch control. Additional lighting comes from three low-voltage LED striplights in the roof.

A three-quarter rock-and-roll bed/ rear seat also has a large auxiliary battery, speakers and 240V socket in its base. Dining is provided by a circular, chrome, pedestal-leg removable table. Facing this is an additional single

ABOVE: Modern Smev sink and hob units, with heat-resistant smoked glass tops, are inset into the worktop and follow the lines of the cabinets.
BELOW: The large capacity three-way fridge has a door finished to match the cabinets.

ABOVE: The buddy seat folds up to create more floor space. Note the pocket and shelf storage built into the end of the seat, and the additional storage under it.

folding buddy seat mounted in a unit on the bulkhead behind the passenger, which also has a shelf and handy open storage box by the sliding door. The buddy seat was originally a Bluebird customs kit, which has been extended and enlarged by welding extra length to the frame. The frame legs have been sprayed silver to match the trim on doors and cabinets.

The bulkhead unit that the buddy seat is attached to contains what is probably one of the most innovative features of the interior: a remote control,

BELOW: Switches for television operation and lights are sited conveniently on the end of the unit by the rear seat/bed.

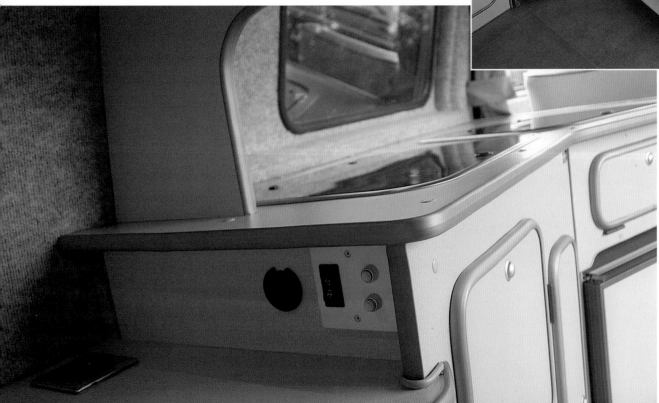

ABOVE: A large hanging closet in the rear can be accessed from the rear or the side.

BELOW: The cushions for the three-quarter rock-and-roll bed have been individually shaped to run flush to the cabinets. Side walls and roof are lined with silver-grey trim to harmonize and provide insulation.

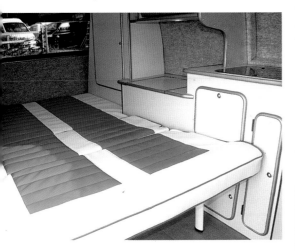

RIGHT: A built-in microwave is something normally reserved for smart motor homes! Note the finishing details such as chrome spotlights, LED lighting strips, and shelves at the side of the microwave.

motorized 15in flat screen television/DVD/Freeview that is operated by a switch by the rear seat. One touch of the switch and the top of the bulkhead unit flips up and the television glides up into position, mounted on a tilt/swivel stand to optimize its viewing position. When it's time for bed, simply touch the switch again and the television slides down out of sight and the top gently closes!

The cabinets are finished in an up-to-the-minute style, with Graffiti Grey cabinets and contrasting Silver Grey trim edging for doors and units, combined with silver push-lock handles. Rounded door corners soften the straight lines of the cabinets, and the slate tile-effect vinyl flooring and silver-grey trim finish of the interior panels and headliner blend in well with the whole colour scheme, making for a contemporary, clean look.

The rear seating and split single/double seats in the cab have been upholstered in light grey leather-look Evolve vinyl to harmonize with the rest of the interior – but to bring in a touch of colour and echo the exterior paint, the centre panels have finished in Eden Green, with matching green piping. The panels have been stitched to break up the otherwise smooth lines. The use of a bright green for contrast lifts and brightens the whole interior, making for a very distinctive, modern look.

The end result is a very modern twist on the VW camping interior: the classic clean lines and neutral, calm greys are emphasized by the bold use of bright green, the circular table opens the living space allowing for easy access to the kitchen areas and for dining, and the microwave and motorized hide-away television raise camping in style to a new level!

family friendly
1959 Kombi

LEFT: The interior has been designed to maximize living space, and the use of pastel yellow door fronts and oak woodwork, combined with cream leather upholstery and coordinating check curtains, gives a contemporary feel to a classic look.

BELOW: A folding buddy seat is fixed to the small unit behind the passenger seat. The unit also contains the additional buddy seat and table leg, as well as keeping the church key safe and providing a handy bottle opener. The top lifts up to reveal useful storage for items such as cameras and books.

When James and Sarah Rowley bought this 1959 Kombi in May 2006 it was basically a party bus: the interior consisted of a full width rock-and-roll bed, a couple of big amps, and a sub-woofer. However, it had been upholstered in cream leather, and all the door and interior panels had been re-covered, so to them it was the perfect opportunity to design an interior that suited their family needs. They started by drawing up two lists. The *must have* list included sleeping for four, fridge, stereo, leisure battery/hook-up, and plenty of storage, especially for the children's things! The *wish* list had cooker/grill, sink, DVD player/TV, and eating space for four. Two questions drove them: what do we like, and where might it go? Sarah says it was like trying to fit a Winnebago into a broom cupboard!

Then, during a week's holiday in the bus, they began to finalize decisions, and James sat down to draw up an isometric sketch of the emerging layout and ideas. As the bus was a walk-

BELOW: The cooker and fridge use push-on gas connectors, making them easily removable for outside use.

The cab retains its stock feel. Note finishing details such as coordinating carpets and leather stereo surround, and gear and handbrake boots that match the side panels.

ABOVE: The lift-out storage boxes are a neat touch; they are on sliders for ease of use. There is additional storage underneath these.

through model, they decided the best option was to have the units down one side, following the classic Devon Moonraker-style layout and incorporating buddy seats, and that a three-quarter rock-and-roll bed would fit best with this layout to maximize space; it would also mean no fiddling around laying out bed boards! They discarded the idea of a sink as it took up too much space, and decided a demountable fridge would maximize space when they were camped up, as that could stand in the awning.

James did not fancy a self-build as the shapes were awkward, and none of the DIY kits around matched their ideas in terms of layout or finish. They were recommended to contact Tim and Vaughn of Custom Classic and Retro, and after seeing some of their work, were happy to entrust the build to them.

Tim talked through their plans and suggested things that would improve their ideas. They decided to use oak frames and oak veneer ply for a traditional look, set off with cupboard and drawer fronts in a pastel cream yellow to create a modern, sunny feel. Minor improvements to their original plans evolved as the build took shape: for example, the lift-out storage boxes on

BELOW: The table is stored under the roof locker, which also has swivel spotlights mounted on both sides.

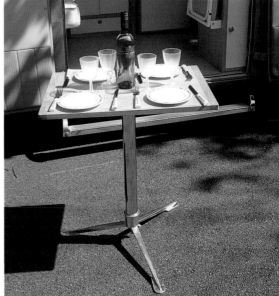

ABOVE: The units are arranged down one side in classic later Moonraker style, providing plenty of worktop space. Note the cut-outs in the seat base for the speakers.

LEFT: With the extra buddy seat clipped in place, a family of four can dine inside in comfort.

the side of the rear seat are now on sliders to make lifting in and out easier, and there is plenty of additional storage below them. The unit behind the passenger seat can be accessed from the top or the side and stores the table leg, additional buddy seat and also the church key, as well as having handy and easily accessible top storage.

The demountable two-way fridge runs off gas or electricity and uses push-on gas connectors to make life easy. It can be used in the awning and also in the home for parties and so on. When it is removed whilst camping, shelves slot into the space left – ideal for wellies and children's toys! The cooker is also removable for outside use, creating plenty of interior space.

They decided against a table that fixed inside, again opting for the flexibility of a free-standing table that can be used inside or out. The top is fitted to a Fiamma leg pole and tripod base, and when not in use the table is stored in the roof at the rear – its size was determined by the space left after fitting a sub-woofer at the side! For interior dining the two buddy seats (sourced from Bluebird as a kit) clip together making space for four – as on the original wish list! A Devon-style roof cabinet and rear toiletry cupboard continue the Moonraker influence, and the buddy seats also make an ideal step to the child's cab bunk!

Initially they toyed with the idea of new upholstery throughout, but it

ABOVE: The table is mounted on a chrome pedestal, Fiamma leg pole, giving flexibility of use.

BELOW: When the fridge is removed, shelves slot into the space to create useful storage when camped up.

Interior colours and curtains coordinate with the exterior colours and give an airy, contemporary look.

seemed a shame to waste the lovely leather that was already in place, so they asked Vaughn to cut down the full rear cushions to three-quarter size and cover the buddy seat set to match, as well as making the cab carpets. The finishing touch of plaid curtains in harmonizing colours was provided by VW Curtains, the yellows coordinating with the colour chosen for the cupboard fronts.

Family entertainment was built in from the start, and the drop-down DVD player is ideal for keeping the children happy when travelling and for wet days on the campsite, whilst the speakers and amps for grown-up music are discreetly sited under the rear seat, as is a pair of 12V sockets. The flooring is commercial, hard-wearing vinyl, much more practical for family camping than carpets.

The end result is an interior that does everything James and Sarah want, with their favourite part being the buddy seats and small front unit. The flexibility of having a removable fridge and cooker, and a free-standing table, suits their needs perfectly, and although influenced by Devon, this design shows how ideas from different sources can be successfully brought together. The sliding removable storage boxes and the slot-in shelving for the fridge space are especially inventive, and everything has its own place, whether children's toys, toiletries or kitchen utensils. The light modern colours and materials harmonize perfectly with the external colours, and are easy to keep clean as well as being modern looking and stylish.

the Summerell Spartan
1986 Panel Van

The absence of side windows means that the humble panel van is rarely first choice for conversion to a camper, and although after-market windows can be fitted, they don't have the factory look. Rather than spoil the clean outside lines, owner Keith Summerell decided to keep the classic look of a panel van and fit a stylish utilitarian interior.

This 2.1 petrol engine T3 started life as a builder's van back in 1986. Originally finished in White, by 2006 it was showing signs of a hard life; but it offered Keith a sensibly priced starting point for something to get out and about in. He wanted a bus that would carry his camping gear and equipment associated with his love of biking and surfing, but also that would enable him to enjoy the great outdoors with a little

more comfort. With this in mind he set about designing what he really needed for a weekend van that would be affordable, practical and clean-looking, and would suit his lifestyle.

After tidying up the van and respraying it in metallic Silver Blue, he turned his attention to fitting out the interior. There did not seem to be much around that was suited to T3 interiors – but then he came across Matt Gregg's website, and liked the look of an interior that Matt had just developed, and which fitted his needs. However, although the basic design ideas offered a starting point, Keith was also clear about modifications and changes he wanted; in discussion with Matt, he designed the interior specifications for Matt to build.

ABOVE: A removable buddy seat provides space for storage or a porta potti.
LEFT: Blue/grey modern pattern fabric harmonizes with interior and exterior colours, and the cream base lightens the enclosed interior.

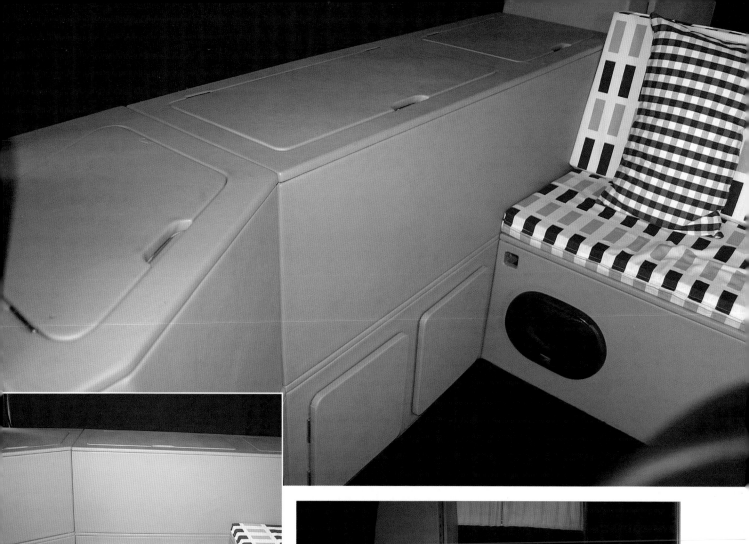

TOP: *The side unit runs from behind the driver, and angles in from the gangway to run along the side wall.*

ABOVE: *Cabinets are built from MDF and have been covered with grey vinyl for a contemporary look and soft feel.*

RIGHT: *The seat base, also covered in grey vinyl, is a three-quarter rock-and-roll bed with speakers sited in the base.*

The van is always used with an awning for camping, so Keith felt no need for a built-in cooker or sink unit, meaning he would have more space for storage. He did not want to alter the clean lines of the van by cutting in side windows, nor did he wish to lose the walk-through cab, but he did want the rear seat to double as a bed. As he likes reading in bed there would also need to be soft lighting in the rear to compensate for lack of natural light, and a sound system.

The interior was built from MDF frames, but instead of wood ply, Keith chose to have all the units covered in soft grey vinyl, which would be hard-wearing, would wipe clean, and also harmonize with the exterior colour. It also makes for a soft and tactile interior surface. A long unit runs down the side opposite the load door, which meets a full height, Westfalia Joker-style hanging closet at the rear. The unit has a sub-woofer sited at one end and large, lined storage compartments accessible from the top or the front. The top of the unit provides shelf space or can be used as a table/worktop.

A double seat runs across the rear, and can be converted to a bed by laying the rear seat back down to meet the seat base; more speakers are sited here. The top of the engine compartment forms part of the bed and has a separate, matching vinyl-covered board for the cushions to sit on; a section of this slides out to allow access to the engine cover plate.

A small removable buddy seat, angled to keep access as wide as possible, sits behind the passenger seat. This doubles for a seat in the awning as well

Porsche seats trimmed in grey velour keep the interior colour scheme consistent.

as providing additional storage or a porta potti space.

Twin reading spotlights (with switches mounted on the wardrobe for ease of use at night) are mounted in the roof at the rear, and a custom lighting twist is provided by the use of red and blue LED lights mounted on the sidewall above the long storage units. A hanging curtain screens the cab area to make for privacy at night.

Keith chose the fabric to blend with the colour scheme – he wanted something that would harmonize with both the interior and exterior colours, and the silver grey and dark blue rectangles on a cream base lift and lighten the interior. The fabric is soft but hard-

wearing, and the covers are also removable and washable. Matching shaped pillow curtains and two scatter cushions finished in navy/white check set off the stylish look. Keith also covered the door cards in grey industrial needlecord carpet, complemented with custom window-winder handles sourced at a show.

Initially he had been unsure about how the interior would work with light sources only from the front and back, but he has found that it feels cosy and warm, and not at all claustrophobic. The van has also been fully insulated, and the roof and walls are lined with grey carpet, which means there are no condensation problems in the mornings.

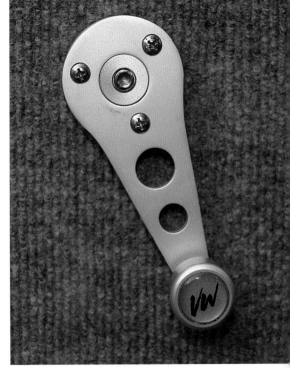

ABOVE: Cab door panels are trimmed in grey needlecord carpet and are set off with matching custom window-winders.
LEFT: A 12in sub-woofer is sited in the base of the side cabinet.

ABOVE: Soft grey, cream and blue interior colours harmonize well with the Silver Blue exterior.

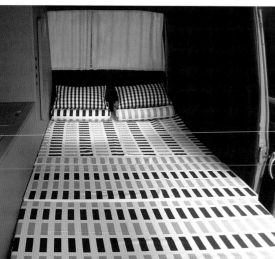

It has the added bonus of making the van much quieter when travelling!

At the moment, entertainment is provided via an Alpine amp and Kenwood head unit feeding two 6 × 9 JBL speakers and a 12in Maranz subwoofer, powered by the leisure battery; but soon to be fitted is a flip-down television/DVD player!

Keith describes the look as 'Spartan – basic, not flashy, but roomy and practical.' The interior may be more utilitarian than others, but Keith wanted something that was in keeping with the working panel van heritage. The interior has proved so successful, and has generated so much interest at VW shows, that it has now been added to MGR's interior range, and named 'The Summerell' after Keith, who inspired and designed the look that Matt has created for him.

LEFT: The rear seat pulls out to make for a full-length roomy bed.

BELOW: The large rear wardrobe is similar in design to that found on Westfalia Jokers. Red and blue LED lights are just visible at top centre. Note shaped pillow cushions.

22

Zombie Kombi
1959 Australian Kombi

LEFT: The rough exterior hides a hand-made oak interior that lovingly reproduces the 1959 Devon layout. The original Australian registration plate has been preserved and mounted on the side wall.

BELOW: A period Thermos petrol cooker, similar to the Enders models used with early Westfalia campers, stands on a folding shelf ready for use.

Not everyone wants a shiny bus or a custom paint job – for Mike and Susie Johnson a bus that is testament to its working life and carrying all its battle scars is as desirable as any concours winner. And although this bus may look scarred on the outside, the inside is a different matter! The bus started life in Australia in 1959, and spent the next forty or so years doing the bidding of various hard taskmasters. When Mike and Susie spotted it for sale they knew it was something they wanted to try and breathe new life into, and the result, though still a work in progress, is a bus with an interior to die for.

Most sellers would have advertised it as the perfect 'blank canvas' (as if that somehow made the bus more desirable!) because the interior was empty, and being a Kombi base model, came with no interior panels or headlining: Mike termed it 'as bare as Mother Hubbard's cupboard'. Mike was happy with the exterior look of the bus, but he and Susie were agreed that the interior would have to be something that would be in keeping with its heritage, but family friendly – and also eye-catching!

They started by trawling the web and collecting hundreds of interior pictures; they also found *VW Camper: The Inside Story* (The Crowood Press), which was excellent for period information and pictures. Initially nothing was rejected: original, repro kits and custom interiors

ABOVE: Wood-ply panelling has been used to face door and interior panels, a style pioneered by Westfalia for their early campers.

ABOVE: The extra cushion base needed to make up the bed is stored in the rear and can double as a small child's bed.

BELOW: Open plaid fabric in pastel shades keeps the early Westfalia styling theme, and also brings a little colour into the interior. The table with wooden legs is an exact copy of how Devon styled them in 1959.

were all carefully looked at, but gradually they began to focus on creating an interior that would fit with the age of the bus. Early Westfalia SO23s, Devons and Canterbury Pitt models all had features they liked, especially the craftsmanship of the wood interiors, and this became their inspiration for a period-style interior that would draw on features from different conversions, as opposed to copying just one.

One of the most distinctive and unique features of early Westfalia campers is the wood-panelled roof and walls, which creates a warm, country cottage feel. Once Mike had seen what this looked like for real, he knew this was the look he wanted. As the bus was right-hand drive, he decided to combine this with the early Devon-style wood interiors. Nearby fellow Split enthusiasts Malc and Abby Bradley just happened to have an original 1959 Devon camper undergoing restoration, and they kindly lent Mike the interior so that he could get it copied. The distinctive feature of these early Devons is polished oak woodwork and a craftsman-built, curved side cabinet, now rarely seen and highly sought after. The interior was taken to a good friend, cabinet maker Tim Clover of

ABOVE: *Another distinctive feature of early Devons is the storage compartments, with slide-down doors, behind the rear seat back.*
LEFT: *Chrome butterfly hinges keep the period styling of the interior.*

Hadleigh, who then set about making templates and building a faithful copy, using oak-faced ply over a pine frame to keep the weight down. The wood was sourced from the local timber merchants, whilst the chrome butterfly hinges came from the local hardware store.

All this would be in keeping with their main idea: something simple, basic and period that would not look out of place on the sun-scorched, travel-worn Aussie bus. It sounds straightforward, but of course it wasn't that simple! Fitting the wood panel headlining turned out to be a major job (Mike has still to finish the rear section). They also totally underestimated the work

involved to reproduce the Devon interior (so much so that Tim has vowed 'never again'!) and the initial budget was soon blown out of the water. Every piece had to be individually measured, cut and shaped, and the curved side cabinet was apparently a nightmare to get right. The end result, however, is just stunning, with the texture and colour of polished oak creating a cosy, warm and inviting feel. Sitting in the interior harks back to a time when life was

much simpler, and love and attention went into hand-built furniture. And of course, wood actually gets better with age.

Initially they had not planned to replace the faded brown gingham fabric that came with the Kombi, mainly because they had got used to seeing it in there, but when they went shopping for bits, Mike was drawn to a pastel green and pink plaid fabric and preferred the idea of adding a little colour,

RIGHT: *The early Devons maximized use of space for storage, as can be seen here in the seat base and back. The original style of water container cabinet has been faithfully reproduced, though finding a correct water container may well be a problem.*

ABOVE: There is nothing quite like the warm, mellow tones of natural wood for a classic feel. The legendary curved side cabinet used on early Devons harks back to the days of hand-built craftsmanship.

ABOVE: Like the interior panels, the headlining has also been finished in wood ply, as were the early Westfalias.

RIGHT: Polished oak cabinets, combined with wood-lined roof and interior panels, bring together period Westfalia and Devon styling and designs to create a warm, cosy interior. The small check used for the curtains and scatter cushions is in the same colours as the seat covers.

but keeping that period look. Foam for the seats came from a local upholsterer in Southampton, and whilst Mike made all the covers, Susie ran up the curtains and scatter cushions, in smaller plaid, to match. Plans to fit classic red and white Marley floor tiles in the traditional check pattern were also abandoned when they spotted a roll of apple green marmoleum on eBay – not only did it harmonize well with the fabric, it was also a bargain price!

The original early Devons had a door-mounted cooker and cabinet. This has not been added, which creates a little extra space inside, especially when the bed is made up. Instead, an old petrol Thermos stove on a door-mounted shelf provides cooking facilities. And

although an original style of bulkhead cabinet for the water container has been fitted, Mike thinks it will be a long search to find an original Devon water container to fit in the space. Plans for the future are to make an overhead locker at the rear of the bus, similar to later Devons.

What they have ended up with is an interior that pays homage to, and is in keeping with, late 1950s styling and materials, which is practical and eye-catching, and works by understatement, in keeping with the whole concept of a bus that has come back from the dead.

Hence the name Zombie Kombi.
(Photographs courtesy of Phil Osborne and Mike Johnson)

green days
1971 Bay Camper

RIGHT: *Green and white are the main interior colours, with white cabinets and green upholstery, and curtains that coordinate with the exterior paint scheme. The wood-panel roof with white trim reverses the cabinet design.*

LEFT: *A radio flyer has been finished to match, complete with coordinating cerise scatter cushions.*

When Shaun Randall and Lisa Bewley-Randall acquired their dream bus it was little more than a shell – no engine, no windows, no interior and lots of rot. From the outset, however, they had a plan to create something striking, stylish and modern that would allow them to use their artistic talents and love of colour to the full. Lisa had already decided on a green colour scheme before they had even found a suitable project bus, and although this one needed extensive work, they knew that

with imagination and hard work they could turn their dreams into reality. Eventually, after many hours of graft and with the help of Elvis the welder, Gavin and Dave the mechanic, the bus was finally ready for paint.

Lisa had already chosen VW Cyber Green because she wanted the bus to match her beloved New Beetle, and Shaun added a personal artistic touch with an airbrushed design in subtle greens, based on the Hokusai classic picture *The Great Wave* on the rear side

panels. The mild custom look is developed with clean lines at the front, a Volkswagen cut-out for the air intake, and Empi 5 spokes and bumpers finished in New Beetle Metallic Grey.

Before an interior layout was decided, Lisa and friend Anna toured the fabric shops, sourcing green chenille-style cotton whipcord from a factory outlet, and rolls of vinyl in veined dark green and marbled ivory from Dunelm for the interior's base colours to coordinate with the Cyber Green exterior.

ABOVE: Interior panels in veined dark green vinyl have a subtle stitched pattern; black handles and speaker surround match the dash and cab carpets.

LEFT: Colour is brought in with a striped throw in cerise, green, white and brown, which harmonizes with all the interior colours, and matching scatter cushions enhance the colour palette. Note finishing details such as the small flower on the cushions, the green glass bud vase and the VW logo on the door panel.

After trawling the shows, they decided the interior layout of the Westfalia Campmobile was a good starting point, with units either side of the gangway and a swivel table mounted on a seat base under the window, and commissioned Kustom Interiors to make up cabinets to their own design.

The unit by the load door has a hinged lid and has been built to fit the cooker (in green, naturally), with a shelved, twin-door crockery and utensil cupboard and gas bottle storage underneath. Opposite this is another unit with a stainless-steel sink and pump tap, also with storage under. Next to this, under the windows, is a single small seat cupboard that meets a full-width rear seat/pull-out (rock-and-roll) bed. The chrome-leg swivel

LEFT: Cabinets are finished in white gloss with a slight textured appearance. Varnished wood edges to doors and worktops add contrast, and flush chrome handles make for a contemporary look.

BELOW: Cab seats have been upholstered in dark green vinyl to match the interior panels. An ivory stripe to match the upper wall lining, and green/white VW logo, add personal styling touches. The black carpeting in the cab coordinates with the dash and door furniture, and the chromed steering column and Empi shifter echo the chrome table leg.

green days: 1971 Bay Camper

RIGHT: *Colour-coordinated accessories include period-style green melamine cutlery and crockery set, glass nightlight holders, matching tablecloths and napkins and green glassware. The table has a hinged extension flap to double the usable area.*

ABOVE: *A single seat under the window is ideal for storing clothes. There is more storage under the rear seat base, which also contains the speakers.*

table is mounted on the single seat base, and can rotate to a variety of positions; it also has a hinged extension leaf that folds out to make for a larger table-top area. A roof locker provides additional storage, and its rear aspect is an open storage area, accessed from the tailgate.

The units were built from MDF, which Shaun has roller painted in white gloss for a slightly textured effect. The worktop edges and door surrounds were kept unpainted, and have been varnished to provide a wood trim contrast effect; chrome flush handles from IKEA add contemporary styling. Backs of doors and worktops are also varnished, adding to the wood 'feel'. The roof has been lined with 3mm matching varnished ply, inspired by early Westfalia interiors, and the colour design of the cabinets is matched in reverse, with the use of white trim on varnished wood, set off with a white, circular roof light.

Lisa and Anna have upholstered the whole interior themselves. Seat cushions are fitted with removable whip-

cord covers and piped edges; for door and interior panels they have used a dark green vinyl in a subtle stitch pattern. The upper sections round the windows and in the rear have been finished in contrasting ivory, keeping the green and white palette consistent, and pastel green curtains with ivory ties add to the overall effect. Lisa has also reupholstered the cab seats in matching stitch-pattern green with ivory stripes for contrast, and for a neat finishing detail the small green and white VW logos are carried through to the sliding door and tailgate panels. The cab and kick panel are carpeted in black to match the dash and door handles and door-mounted speakers; another styling detail is the use of Metallic Grey on sections of the dash top and sides to harmonize with the wheels and bumpers.

Additional colour has been brought in with a striped seat throw in cerise, green, brown and white to coordinate with all the interior colours, and scatter cushions in cerise, green and the

ABOVE: *Green, circular non-slip mats, melamine crockery and kettle are all part of the attention to detail; even the 1970s-style tray, with cerise flowers, matches the colour scheme.*
BELOW: *The cooker, in dark green, is kept in the cabinet by the load door with a large, twin-door, shelved storage cupboard underneath.*

ABOVE: The roof has been lined with varnished wood ply, with a white trim detailing that reverses the cabinet design. A flip-down television/PlayStation provides entertainment on those increasingly frequent wet summer days.

LEFT: The unit behind the driver has a pump tap and stainless-steel sink. All the insides of the doors and worktops are varnished wood to match the edging.

striped fabric add the unified effect. The flooring brings in a garden feel of lawn and decking, with grass-pattern tiles edged with wood-look vinyl.

Matching accessories have been used to full effect with green glass bud vases from B & Q, pale green circular non-slip mats for worktops from IKEA, pale green melamine crockery, and matching kettle, green and cerise glass nightlight holders, green glassware and coordinated table cloths and napkins – and even a model New Beetle in Cyber Green being just some of the colour-coordinating period accessories Lisa

has sourced from interior design and charity shops.

It took about eighteen months to get the bus looking how they wanted, and it has been a real team effort, with friends Elvis, Anna, Dave and Gavin all working hard to help Shaun and Lisa create something distinctive and per-sonal. Modern styling works alongside period detailing to make for a crisp, coherent look, and the addition of a flip-down television mounted in the cab roof, and a modern sound system, bring in up-to-the-minute technology and contemporary design.

ABOVE: A Westfalia-style swivel-leg table is fitted to the single seat base and can pivot to a variety of positions for use.

BELOW: In keeping with the white and green theme, marbled ivory vinyl has been used for the upper panel sections and window surrounds. The cushion covers are removable, with brown buttons to echo the use of wood in the interior. The rear of the roof locker has an open storage area. Note more matching accessories!

a bus for all seasons
2006 T4 LWB Kombi

When the Kombi was introduced in 1951 it quickly established its credentials as the first MPV (multi-purpose vehicle), its removable row of seats and its side widows allowing it to be used as both transporter and people carrier. The model name 'Kombi' is still used by VW on its latest T5 range, and the modern Kombi basically follows the same interior design principles as its 1950s predecessor (though much more luxurious in styling and trim than the utilitarian original versions), with removable seating to create load space.

However, Guy Luard's T5 Kombi adds a whole new dimension to the concept, because it now also has a fully removable camping interior, meaning the bus can be load hauler, people carrier or camper. Guy's brief to Simon Weitz of Interior Motive was quite simple: design and build a camping interior that was easy to install and remove, with the kitchen area in the rear allowing him to sit and enjoy an early morning cup of tea whilst his partner could carry on sleeping!

The floor has been built from 18mm MDF, faced with Lava pattern Marmoleum, and is in three interlocking sections that bolt to the van floor. The furniture is secured to the floor using easy-to-use wingnuts. Two single box seats sit behind the cab seats, with lift

ABOVE: The kitchen area, with cooker, fridge and large table/worktop area, is sited in the rear. The birch-ply cabinet is topped with pale blue laminate.

LEFT: The interior is designed to be easily removable, with two single seats and a rear bench in the living area.

LEFT: *Curving lines create a sense of space and modernity, and the cooker is in an open, built-in recess, also faced with blue laminate.*
BELOW: *A narrow gangway enables walkthrough access between kitchen and living areas.*

tops to access storage, and a single bench seat faces these. This has storage compartments at each end for the bed boards and fittings, and three pull-out box sections that provide storage or additional seating for use in an awning. There is another cupboard in the rear of the seat back.

Cabinets have been built from birch ply and finished in clear satin lacquer to keep the interior light, and all units feature a stainless-steel plinth base, adding a modern styling detail. The bed is constructed by first laying down boards between the seats; as the interior had to be removable, this was a better method than fitting a rock-and-roll bed.

A low side unit runs from the sliding door to the rear, with two lift-top

RIGHT: *A large-capacity Waeco fridge sits in the centre. Note how the flowing lines are maintained by the curving side corners to the cabinet.*
BELOW: *Two push-lock curved doors reveal more storage for a gas bottle and kitchen utensils.*

ABOVE: Seat and scatter cushions are upholstered in blue/cream stripe fabric to harmonize with the natural wood and blue laminate.

LEFT: Twin buddy seats are sited behind the front cab seats, so the walkthrough runs from the cab right into the rear.

storage compartments, and a narrow gangway between this and the rear seat and kitchen unit maintains walkthrough access between the living and rear areas. The unit has been given a worktop of Peaceful Blue laminate, bringing some colour into the interior; it can also double as a seat.

As the vehicle is a long wheel-base version, there is plenty of space in the rear, which has been designed as the kitchen area with cooker, storage and Waeco fridge. There is a large worktop/table area, also finished in Peaceful Blue laminate, with the cooker inset into a recessed area; beneath it is storage space for a gas bottle and utensils, accessed by twin curved doors. The cabinet curves round from the door edge to meet the fridge, and the flowing curves create a sense of space, whilst push-catch cupboard operation keeps the lines unbroken and clean.

The grey of the fridge front harmonizes with the Kombi interior panel finish, and touches such as the manufacturer's name in blue matching with the blue laminate worktops, tie the design together. The use of curves, stainless-steel plinth and light natural wood

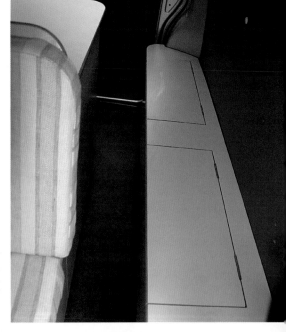

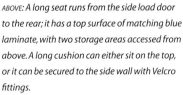

ABOVE: A long seat runs from the side load door to the rear; it has a top surface of matching blue laminate, with two storage areas accessed from above. A long cushion can either sit on the top, or it can be secured to the side wall with Velcro fittings.

LEFT: As the furniture is designed to be fully removable, the bed is constructed by laying down boards between the seating.

a bus for all seasons: 2006 T4 LWB Kombi

LEFT: Storage sections for table boards and fittings have been built into each end of the rear bench.

BELOW: The three storage boxes slide out and can be used for seats in an awning.

makes for a very contemporary look, and the unit's matching blue laminate used as a worktop and to line the cooker recess is echoed in the seat upholstery, which is finished in pale blue and cream stripe fabric.

Future plans include a rear awning so the kitchen can be used more effectively, and a table using one of the bed boards. The original Kombi bench seat has been retained and can be easily fitted once the camping set-up is removed, making for true multi-purpose use for leisure and work – the original concept behind the creation of the Kombi model.

LEFT: There is additional storage for bedding and clothes in the base of each buddy seat, and in three lift-top box storage units in the bench seat.

BELOW: Birch ply has been finished with satin lacquer to maintain the light tones of the wood. Note the stainless-steel plinth base, and the way the unit corners are gently curved instead of angular.

25

Torvette restyle
1967 Devon Torvette Spaceway

LEFT: *Original Devon-style units, as in the single seat with storage under and at the back, have been mixed with new styles of unit such as the cooker cabinet. Light Canadian ply has been used to face the cabinet work, with contrasting dark hardwood for the tops and edges.*

BELOW: *The cooker unit features a slide-out shelf/ worktop, utensil drawer and storage cupboards.*

Whilst some people opt for the stock interior route, and others for a radical redesign, another route is to adapt and update a classic design, as in the case of this 1967 Devon Spaceway Torvette. The Torvette was the budget model, and instead of the swing-out Caravette-style cooker, had a cooker sited behind the single seat by the door. This particular version had the added bonus of the optional Dormobile roof fitted in the Devon factory.

When Dave Sutherland acquired the camper it was in a very sorry state – the paint was dull and faded, and the interior, although intact, was damp and

BELOW: The original twin-door Torvette rear unit has been cut down to allow for more sleeping space when the bed is made up.

ABOVE: The hardwood cabinet-trim styling is carried through in the rear, and the side sections of the roof panelled in matching ply.

BELOW: A new unit, sited at the end of the rear seat, provides more storage and a handy shelf/table top.

ABOVE: The exterior colours are carried through into the interior with seat cushions covered in green/white open plaid, and scatter cushions and curtains finished in matching smaller check. The sisal carpet edges are overlocked in green, and arm-rest cushions on the rear seat make for a settee look.

mouldy and the fittings were rusting. The wood veneer on the cabinets was splitting and peeling, carpet tiles had been glued to all the door panels and roof, and the pop-top canvas had more holes than a tea strainer! Dave decided it was pointless to try and refurbish the cabinets; instead he took the opportunity to keep the traditional Devon styling and wood finish, but to update it to recreate the period feel with contemporary styling touches and to adapt the layout to suit his own needs.

Jane, Dave's wife, was fully involved in helping the design evolve, and her first suggestion was to replace the bed (made by laying boards) with a three-quarter rock-and-roll bed, which would leave enough room for a side cabinet. They also decided to remove the bunks in the Dormobile roof to provide more headroom and create the feeling of light and space. Taking inspiration from Westfalia wood-panelled interiors, Dave has lined the cab roof with flexible ply, and the side sections of the main roof in rigid ply.

Dave commissioned 'Buff the Chippie' to build new cabinets to his specifications. Light Canadian ply to match the roof has been used, with a darker hardwood trim for contrast. The hardwood is used to top and edge all the units: as well as being more durable

A small, portable storage box sits in the gangway, and is a useful place to store sunglasses, cameras, maps and other essentials.

and harder wearing, it is also very pleasing to the eye. The back was also lined with ply, and the original style of Torvette rear cabinet was cut down to a single door unit to allow more room to lay out the rock-and-roll bed. The Devon-style hanging closet in the rear has been kept, and instead of facing the cupboard doors with black melamine, as was the practice on 1960s Devons, the doors are plain wood to lighten the interior. Chrome handles, catches and hinges are used on all the cabinets.

The single seat behind the driver has retained the original Devon design, but has a much smaller back cushion to make for easy access to the bulkhead storage compartment. Instead of a second single seat with the cooker sited behind it, Dave decided to design a completely new unit for the cooker, which incorporates a pull-out work surface, two cupboards and a utensil drawer. He also redesigned the side unit, which originally contained the coolbox, as a two-cupboard unit to provide more storage space with a wood shelf top so you can stand a table lamp and period radio on it, or cups of tea when you are in bed! A handy, small, portable box sits in the gangway and is an ideal stowaway place for sunglasses, maps, cameras and other essentials.

Dave and Jane decided to keep the 1960s pastel shades for the exterior, but opted for Leguan Gruen (LH6E, a late 1970s VW colour) and Pearl White for something that was in period, but different to the usual Velvet Green and white combination.

Jane then set about creating the interior look to complement the exterior colours and styling. The driver and passenger seat covers and door cards were upholstered in cream faux leather with green piping on the seats. Other seating and the rock-and-roll bed cushions were made with 4in (10cm) foam covered in a green and cream-checked cotton fabric, with a colour

ABOVE: Pleated cream interior panels with chrome trim match those on the cab doors. The single seat back cushion has been made smaller to allow easy access to the bulkhead storage compartment.

RIGHT: Cream faux leather interior panels, with Microbus-style chrome trim and cream seat covers with green piping, give a light, airy feel to the cab.

ABOVE: The interior has a light, fresh, airy feel that blends period and contemporary design.

The cab roof area is lined in flexible ply to match the cabinets, an interior style pioneered on the early Westfalia campers.

ABOVE: A Devon-style hanging closet in the rear has been retained.
BELOW: The top of the cooker unit also doubles as a table/worktop. Chrome handles, knobs and hinges have been fitted to all the cabinets to bring in a contemporary styling touch.

coordinated smaller checked fabric used for the scatter cushions and curtains. The addition of chrome fittings to the cabinets modernizes the look, whilst the traditional Westfalia-style sisal carpet has been updated by overlocking the edges with a matching green. The light cream upholstery and panels make for a clean, spacious feel, and the addition of chrome Microbus trim on door and side panels ties in with the chrome fittings on the cabinets and the chrome exterior beltline trim.

A new elevating roof and green-striped canvas were purchased from Dormobile in Southampton and fitted by Dave and his brother, after extensive renovation to the original side hinges. In keeping with the 'period, but with a modern twist' theme, Dave has also installed a 1641cc motor, dropped spindles, Safari windows, US spec bumpers, Deluxe body trim, chromed headlight eye shades, a period dashboard radio, and a Westfalia-style roofrack, which had to be remodelled and made smaller to accommodate the elevating roof and carry the spare wheel. Other modifications included fitting a hook-up and leisure battery.

Together, Dave and Jane have recreated an original style look and added modern touches. The classic Devon Torvette interior has been blended with a touch of Westfalia, and tastefully and subtly updated to create a look that feels period but contemporary, and which is light, airy and fresh-looking. And despite winning awards, it isn't just a showpiece – it is used on a regular basis for camping in muddy, waterlogged fields!

(Additional photographs courtesy of Dave Sutherland)

revamping a Viking
1977 Viking Spacemaker

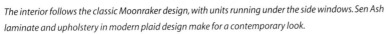

The interior follows the classic Moonraker design, with units running under the side windows. Sen Ash laminate and upholstery in modern plaid design make for a contemporary look.

ABOVE: The cab and interior metal have been painted to match the outside body colours.
BELOW: The single seat is a lift-out box unit, perfect for bulky items or a porta potti.

The Viking conversion featured a rear kitchen, an enormous roof with berths on all sides, and a bed that was laid out across almost all the interior cargo space. As such it was very different from many other conversions around, and the full-length roof made for a spacious interior. Whilst the layout offered a very different and innovative route for 1970s camper interior design, by the time Peter and Pamela Gee acquired this version in 2002 the interior was well past its sell-by date.

They had wanted a camper to use for touring holidays, and for two seasons enjoyed the lifestyle of living with their Viking, Splodge, on holiday. However, they began to think it was time to refit

ABOVE: *Lots of living space is created when the seat is removed.*

ABOVE: *The tops of the side unit lift up to reveal a sink/drainer and twin hob/grill. A modern Easicool unit provides cool storage.*
RIGHT: *The long worktop, finished in brushed aluminium, doubles as a useful shelf/standing area.*

the interior, and took the opportunity to create something they would find more user friendly. They had found the rear kitchen was not very accessible, the cab bunks were awkward and uncomfortable, the hook-up and fridge no longer worked, and laying out the bed was like doing a jigsaw puzzle! Plus the upholstery was tired and faded, the browns and oranges giving a very dated 1970s feel.

Rather than just refurbish the existing interior, they decided to start again to create an interior that would meet their holiday needs and also have a more modern look. They contacted Andy at

VW Curtains, and together they came up with an interior design that would solve the problems of the original layout. A long run of units is sited, Moonraker-style, under the windows, with modern Easicool, pump-tap sink, twin hob/grill, and lots of storage. Sen Ash laminate was chosen for the cabinet work to bring a light, modern look to the interior, with the full-length worktop of the unit finished in brushed aluminium. Doors have curved corners edged with dark grey trim, and the grey edging to the cabinets ties in, making for a clean look.

At the end of the unit is a small cupboard containing a top-mounted

BELOW: *A small hanging closet is situated in the rear, with a small cupboard for electric socket and heater controls to the side, adjoining the main unit.*

ABOVE: *Interior panels and curtains have been finished in the same fabric as the seats/bed cushions.*

LEFT: *The front and rear transverse roof berths have been boxed in to provide storage. Twin spots are mounted under the rear section.*

A fixed cab bunk runs above the windows, and hinges up to create more headroom.

chrome 240V socket and the heater control panel; this continues to a hanging closet in the rear. There is additional storage in a roof cupboard, which also has two spotlights mounted in its base. The bunks have been removed, and a full-length fixed berth built above the kitchen unit; this can be hinged up to maximize headroom, and the spaces round the other three sides of the roof provide more storage when the van is camped up.

A three-quarter rock-and-roll bed doubles as the rear bench seat, and a rectangular pedestal-leg table, edged in dark grey with a brushed aluminium top to match the kitchen unit, is mounted on the floor. Outlets for the Propex heater and another chrome 240V socket are sited in the seat base. The Gees initially considered a single fold-down Devon-style buddy seat to go behind the front passenger seat, but, wanting something more substantial, they decided to have a single box seat with rear cushion mounted on the bulkhead. The base section is removable, making for much more interior space. Although it can hold a porta potti, Peter and Pamela find it very useful for storing bulky items.

Although at first they were dubious about the unique paint scheme with which the bus was attired when they

RIGHT: *Finishing details such as coordinated carpet, dark grey trim to cabinet and door edges, and silver push-button handles, add a modern styling touch.*

BELOW: *The table is floor-mounted on a chrome pedestal leg. Note the additional 240V socket and heater outlets in the seat/bed base.*

first purchased it, they have since become quite attached to it, and it always draws interest and admiring glances wherever they park. In fact the outside pink and green colours, which are also applied to the inside metal and cab area, have been carried through to the interior upholstery scheme: Apple and Wine patchwork fabric, in a bold, open plaid design on a cream base, coordinates perfectly, and makes for a bright, modern look that also complements the finish and contemporary design of the cabinets. The curtains, sliding door panel and rear interior panels have all been trimmed in matching fabric, as have the sections above the side windows, bringing in colour and light. A fitted, hard-wearing industrial carpet, in beige to harmonize with the fabric base colour and cabinet work, unifies the overall look and adds a living-room feel.

The new interior provides more practical and ergonomic use of space, as well as being stylish and modern, and the revamped Viking is set to take them travelling for a long time to come to shows and on holidays.

BELOW: *The Spacemaker roof was one of the biggest selling points for the Viking Camper.*

street rod styling
1958 Kombi

This 1958 Kombi is a real head turner. Finished in Porsche Guard's Red and Audi Brilliant Black, it has been built for performance as well as looks, and features a 1941cc engine with an impressive spec that includes AS 41 full flow crank case, CB performance counter-balanced crank, lightened eight-dowel flywheel, CB straight-cut cam gears, Engle 110 cams, all chrome tin ware, dual twin 44 Weber carbs, stainless Fatboy exhaust, CB atomic oil cooler and external Fram filter. With such an impressive motor and distinctive paint scheme, the interior had to match this high standard!

Owners Peter Moore and Tracey Starkey Moore knew the bus would have to have something a bit special. As it was not going to be used as a traditional camper (that is, with cooking and washing taking place inside) they knew they could dispense with cabinets, and decided comfortable and luxurious seating was what they really wanted. Peter had long been a fan of the look that Boyd Coddington had been designing and fitting in his Hot Rods, and after years of looking at custom cars and street rods, as well as ambling around VW shows, he had

ABOVE: The sumptuous interior is finished in top quality Italian leather, using red and black to coordinate with the exterior paint scheme.
RIGHT: A classic stitch pattern has been used on the seat cushions, which is carried through to the lower sections of the cab, door and side panels.

ABOVE: The seating has been trimmed in tuck and roll style, and is deeply padded for luxury and comfort. Note the way the bulkhead has been finished to match the panels.

a fairly clear idea of what he wanted. The interior had to be in black and red to match the exterior, and freed from the restraints of a camping interior, all he needed was storage under the seats, a rock-and-roll bed, night heater and rear-facing seat DVD screen! Party on!

He set about drawing up some possible layout designs, and he and Tracey quickly decided on tuck-and-roll leather seating, with matching red and black

LEFT: A drop-down Alpine DVD player, fitted on the fresh air intake vent, provides entertainment whilst lounging on the luxurious leather seating.

BELOW: Padded cushioning is carried through in the rear section that forms part of the bed.

ABOVE: *The seat bases have soft curving lines, and the carpeting keeps the colour scheme consistent with matching soft red and black over-locked edging.*

interior panels and plenty of gauges and racing harnesses for the cab, to give that street-rod feel and look. Unlike some designs, the ideas did not change or evolve: once Peter had decided, that was it.

The hardest problem was finding someone who could refurbish the interior to the standard they wanted. After a fruitless search for the rear-facing seat that matched their design, Peter had to break out the woodworking tools and build it himself! Tappers, a local trim shop, upholstered the seats and interior panels, using a stitch pattern with plain black topping on the panels. Finest quality Italian leather was used for that luxurious feel, and details such as the silver Creative Engineering logo doorpulls add to the custom touch.

Entertainment is provided by a drop-down Alpine DVD screen, which is fitted on the cab air vent, and the impressive sound system consists of a Pioneer CD head unit, Genesis 4

The interior upholstery exudes class and style, and is set off with coordinating red and white check curtains.

ABOVE: *The interior panels echo the outside scheme, with the upper sections finished in plain black and the lower sections in red with a stitching pattern to match the seating. Note details such as the coordinating red door check strap.*

ABOVE: A Scat shifter and Simpson racing harnesses, in black and red to match, add to the hot rod-influenced styling. Note the matching red dash grab handle.

LEFT: The cab follows hot-rod styling with chrome Mooneye gauges and gas pedal, and Motolita steering wheel. Attention to styling detail can be seen in the way the kick panels echo the distinctive exterior V shape of a Split bus.

channel 1,000W amplifier, Pioneer 1,200W amplifier, coupled with Boston acoustic pro-series 6.5in component speakers up front, JL Audio 6 × 9 speakers in the rear seat box, and two 8in Boston Acoustic pro-subs in a custom box. So as not to annoy neighbours too much, the whole van has been soundproofed with extreme Dynamat, and for those cold nights to make it even more warm and inviting inside,

an Eberspächer heater keeps them toasty.

The hot-rod look up front has been achieved with Mooneye gauges (sourced direct from California and considered the ultimate in cool street cred) that include electronic speedo, rev counter, fuel gauge, oil temp, oil pressure and time clock, set off with a Motalita steering wheel and Scat shifter. Simpson racing harnesses are

finished in red and black to keep the colour theme and hot rod styling, and the shifter and handbrake boots are finished in matching red leather, with even the dash grab handle coded to match. Another custom touch is the echoing of the distinctive Splitty V front on the front kick panels, and the whole interior is set off with harmonizing check curtains, red carpets edged in black, and red neon lighting for ambience!

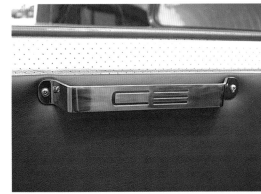

ABOVE: Silver Creative Engineering logo door pulls add to the custom styling.

LEFT: Attention to detail is everywhere in this bus, as can be seen in the matching cab carpeting and the red leather boots for handbrake and shifter.

continental influence
1976 Bay Camper

The interior of this camper has been inspired by the 1972 Westfalia range, in particular the Continental, a right-hand-drive model introduced specifically for the UK market. The most distinctive feature of this interior layout was a cooker sited in the side of the wardrobe, which folded out to sit across the gangway.

The camper was originally a Devon Caravette, with a sink/cooker unit at the end of a three-quarter rock-and-roll bed – but by the time Lee Mitchell acquired it in 2007 it had been drastically modified, with a full-width rear seat/bed and a cabinet running behind the cab seats, meaning the walk-through facility had been lost. Though quite functional it was too small for a family of four, so Lee decided to start

from scratch and build something that would be more 'family friendly'. After stripping out the interior units, the first job was to fit a pair of tan leather Saab seats in the cab so that long journeys would be less tiring.

He then looked carefully through *VW Camper – The Inside Story*, noting ideas that appealed. One layout in particular stood out: the Westfalia Continental, with its cooker that folded out from the wardrobe across the gangway, as it seemed to offer the space and flexibility he wanted by restoring access to the cab and providing plenty of living room. He sat down in the bus with the basic Westfalia plan in mind and, with his daughter, began to sketch out possibilities.

With a clear design drawn out, he then began sourcing materials. He

ABOVE: The tall unit behind the driver is modelled on a Westfalia design; the cooker is located in the top section, with additional storage cupboards under and hanging space at the side.
LEFT: The top door hinges down across the gangway, when the cooker can stand on it.

LEFT: A bottle opener and 240V sockets are mounted on the side.

BELOW: The Franke stainless-steel sink is inset into the unit, and the circular top doubles as a chopping board.

ABOVE: The 40ltr Husky Stella fridge is sited under the sink and can hold thirty-five cans of chilled beer!

BELOW: The full-width rear seat/rock-and-roll bed makes for comfortable and roomy sitting or sleeping space.

wanted something more durable and aesthetic than MDF, and chose Brazilian hardwood ply for the cabinets. This has been coated with matt varnish to bring out the wood grain and lighten the interior, making for a natural look without a reflective gloss shine. No edging has been used, to avoid moisture traps, and clean lines have been maintained by not fitting protruding handles that children can catch themselves on. Instead, circular finger pull holes are used to open doors and cupboards.

The top cupboard of the large unit behind the driver stores the portable twin hob/grill, the door of which hinges down for it to stand on. Below this are two additional storage cupboards, one for crockery, with a larger one below. A wardrobe/hanging space is accessed from the side. The sink and fridge unit is sited by the load door behind the passenger seat, and the cooker door meets this to form a solid base; furthermore, because the cooker is free-standing, the flap-down door can be used as a table or worktop. It is also perfect for the portable entertainment system, which consists of an X Box with high definition and travel pack. As well as game play it has a built-in DVD player, and also a Sky television satellite tuner – and it features surround sound!

continental influence: 1976 Bay Camper

BELOW: Speakers have been sited in the seat base, and the floor is carpeted for a homely living-room feel.

ABOVE: The box seat under the windows contains the mains hook-up, treble 240V socket and power inverters. A 400w electric heater is mounted on the main cabinet, and is perfectly safe as the casing does not get hot.

The Franke sink is a circular under-counter version, and is inset into the unit with a removable wooden work-top that doubles as a chopping board. A 40ltr Husky Stella fridge fits the available space perfectly, and can hold thirty-five cans of beer; it has the added advantages of not needing to be vented, and running silently at night, and it can also run off the battery. On the side of the unit is a bottle opener and twin 240V sockets. A portaloo can fit neatly in the gangway space: with two young daughters this is an essential camping item!

A 400 watt silent-running electric heater is mounted on the side of the main unit by the wardrobe door, and is perfect for keeping the inside warm at night. The two hooks above this are ideal for drying tea towels; there is an interior light mounted above them.

Running under the window from the wardrobe to the rear seat is a box seat, under which is a treble 240V socket, invertors for running the fridge and

LEFT: A unit in the rear provides more cupboard space and two open storage areas, and has been angled to follow the line of the seat back.
BELOW: The roof locker has twin caravan-style sliding doors so that the children have their own areas to access when in their bunks.

ABOVE: *Cabinets are built from Brazilian hardwood ply finished with matt varnish. 32mm circular holes have been used instead of handles to keep clean lines.*

ABOVE: *The gangway flap is also perfect for standing the combined X box and satellite television on.*

BELOW: *Leather seats from a Saab have been fitted in the cab to make for comfortable travelling.*

X Box/television, and the mains hook-up control. The full-width rear seat/bed has been retained, with the base rebuilt in matching Brazilian ply; two speakers have been put here. Lee managed to source two original Devon cab bunks, and has had white vinyl covers made up to match the rear seat upholstery. (The wardrobe unit had to be made slightly lower than the Westfalia version to accommodate a bunk above it.) The roof locker has been replaced with a new version that features twin sliding doors, giving his two girls easy access to their own storage spaces from the bunks. Cup hold-

ers by the rear seat are also used for their personal nick nacks.

A unit in the rear provides more cupboard space and two open storage areas; it has been angled from the front to follow the line of the seat back. Hidden in the base is a safe and secure storage area under a false floor.

Lee has carried out all the interior woodwork and fitments himself, and has found that the layout and design suits his family perfectly. Next on the agenda is a table, which will be a free-standing version using a Fiamma tripod leg; it will store under the roof locker when not in use.

heart of oak
1967 Split Camper

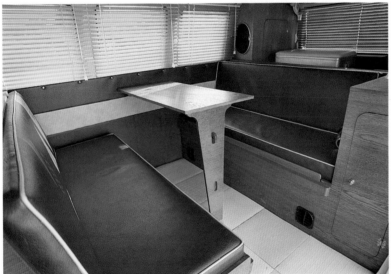

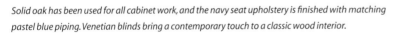

Solid oak has been used for all cabinet work, and the navy seat upholstery is finished with matching pastel blue piping. Venetian blinds bring a contemporary touch to a classic wood interior.

ABOVE: The interior is trimmed in navy vinyl with pastel blue (coordinating with the exterior blue) contrast stripe panels.

This 1967 right-hand-drive camper is believed to have originally been a Danbury conversion, but by the time the previous owner, Thomas Lubbock, acquired it a few years ago it was in a very sorry state. The interior was tatty and incomplete, and the body was rotten in all the usual places – basically the whole bottom 6in (15cm) needed replacing, including sills, corners, outriggers, front and rear valences, tailgate cab doors and engine lid. Tom Lubbock set about restoring the bus inside and out and, rather than take the restore-to-stock route, took the opportunity to follow the classic bus custom street-rod styling trend, with polished Empi 5 spoke wheels, lowered suspension, narrowed front beam and a 1776cc motor. The use of period-style pastels in the modern colours of Diamond Blue under Lotus White adds a contemporary twist to the traditional two-tone colour scheme.

Whilst the exterior styling follows the custom route, the interior pays homage to the early days of Devon styling, with craftsman-built oak units arranged dinette style. As the bus was to be used as a weekender rather than for family holidays, the interior has been designed to maximize storage and sleeping/ dining space; any cooking or washing

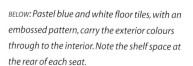

LEFT: *The headliner is finished in coordinating dark grey.*

BELOW: *Pastel blue and white floor tiles, with an embossed pattern, carry the exterior colours through to the interior. Note the shelf space at the rear of each seat.*

can be done in an awning, so those facilities were deemed unnecessary.

The units have been built from solid oak and consist basically of two facing bench seats, with storage under and shelf tops across the rears. To make up the bed, the seat back from the rear bench simply drops down between the two bench bases, which, as well as being very straightforward to do, has the added benefit of making extra leg room. The table is also made from solid oak, and the craftsmanship of the woodwork can be seen in the shaping of the fold-down leg (again, following period Devon styling) and the wooden peg to secure it when folded. For travelling, the table stores in a retaining bracket behind the back of the forward-facing bench, and is held in place with a revolving clip.

At the side of the three-quarter rear bench seat is an oak storage cabinet, accessed from the end by the cargo door. The top forms an excellent shelf/standing area. Twin cabinets, with forward-facing speakers, sit on either side at the rear, and meet a roof locker providing plenty of additional storage space. A Propex heater is located beneath the forward-facing bench and vented to the underside via hot air outlets in the base, with the thermostat conveniently placed to the left of the

BELOW: *The table is also made from solid oak, and the craftsmanship of the woodwork can be seen in the shaping of the fold-down leg (again following period Devon styling) and the wooden peg to secure it when folded.*

The dinette layout takes its inspiration from the first Devons, and there is additional storage in two facing rear cabinets that sit under a full-width roof locker. The complete rear seat back drops down between the benches to make up the bed.

steering wheel so the interior temperature can be controlled for those chilly spring morning drives.

Contemporary styling has been brought in with the use of pale blue vinyl contrast panels in the navy door and side wall panels, and this theme has been carried through with matching blue piping on the navy seat upholstery on both the bench seat cushions and on the cab seats. Grey carpeting has been used for the cab kick panel, with a matching grey floor carpet edged with blue, whilst the pastel blue and ivory-white floor tiles, laid in classic check pattern, bring the exterior colour scheme inside. A dark grey headlining completes the interior look.

Perhaps the most distinctive and original contemporary styling touch is provided by the slatted Venetian blinds fitted to all the side windows and the tailgate window. Finished in matt aluminium, these were all individually made up as a special order by a marine manufacturer in the Midlands, and they add a very modern and individual look to the interior design. They also provide maximum control of interior lighting, from subdued to bright.

Viv John acquired the bus in 2006 because Mr Lubbock was looking for an

ABOVE: Matt aluminium slatted Venetian blinds are fitted to all the side windows and the tailgate window, providing a distinctive and original contemporary styling touch as well as maximizing privacy and natural lighting control.

BELOW: Designed mainly as a 'weekender', the interior is comfortable and spacious as well as stylish.

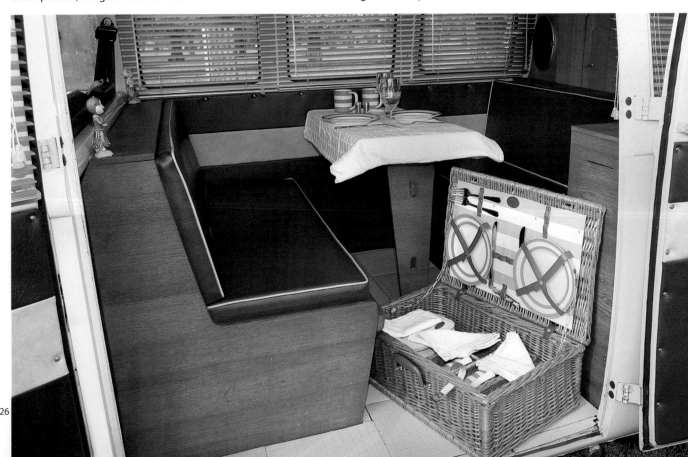

ABOVE: The cab seats are trimmed to match the rear cushions, and the exterior blue has been used to finish the dash and interior metal. Finishing details include the grey kick panel and matching floor mat edged in dark blue.

LEFT: Dash tachograph and oil temperature and pressure gauges continue the custom styling theme.

early Porsche 911. At the time, Viv was the proud owner of a well known silver 1973 911 T/E – so a deal was struck, as Viv had hankered after a bus for some time. (Viv has been into the VW scene for more than fifteen years, and also owns a show-winning Karmann Cabriolet.) The interior suits his needs perfectly, and he says that it's great for days out with friends, but also good for weekends away as it's comfortable and warm and always a talking point at shows!

Since owning the bus Viv has fitted the Propex heater and a Sony CD head unit with Rockford Fosgate speakers and sub-woofer, and plans to fit a drop-down DVD unit, wired to the sound system. In keeping with the custom theme he has also added a Creative Engineering roofrack and a dash tachograph, as well as the necessary oil temperature and pressure gauges, so he can keep an eye on the 1776cc motor from the cab.

Finishing details such as flower garlands on the mirror, chrome bud vase with blue gerbera, and hula monkeys bring in a touch of surfing culture and, of course, humour.

(Photographs courtesy of Viv John and Mike Moore)

RIGHT: Flower garlands and hula girls bring in echoes of Hawaii and surfing culture....

BELOW: ...whilst hula monkeys on the bulkhead shelf add a touch of humour.

127

Devon meets Brazil
1975 Brazilian Fleetline

This split-screen bus was built in Brazil in 1975 as part of the Fleetline programme. VW Brazil used dies and presses from VW Germany, which had been superseded by tooling for their new models, and the Brazilian-built models were a strange combination of older and newer model parts and mixed body styling, coupled with some of VW Brazil's own styling and parts. Production of the twenty-three-window Deluxe (or 'Samba', as it is more commonly known) had ceased in Germany back in 1963, and Bay window models had replaced 'Splitties' in 1967; but this 1975 Brazilian-built Fleetline has pre-1963 Deluxe body style, pre-1955 cargo door handles, a 1961/1962 tailgate, and a Brazilian-made front panel with a pressed VW badge amongst its hybrid mix!

Taking the early 1960s external styling of the bus as his starting point, owner Paul Westfield wanted an interior

RIGHT: The small bulkhead cabinet by the door is for toiletries. A traditional Devon feel is maintained by black laminate doors, but chrome bow handles and trim update the look.

BELOW: The interior has been finished in oak, with oak laminate flooring, coordinated with cream upholstery. Contemporary styling has been introduced with a chrome pedestal table leg and green stripes and piping on the seats.

ABOVE: The roof locker also has chrome trim detailing, and curtains in black/cream/beige open check harmonize with the interior colours.
LEFT: The magazine rack folds down to form part of the bed base, and speaker grills have been discreetly cut into the seat base. The stitched seat cushion design and green piping detail are carried through on interior panels.

ABOVE: There is additional storage behind the front bench seat back.
BELOW: The table is laid down between the seats to form the bed base, as on 1960s Devons.

in keeping with the period. As the bus was originally a Microbus but now an empty shell, returning it to stock was not an option, so here was the chance to create an interior that was as individual as the bus itself. Finding Westfalias of the time rather cluttered inside, he was drawn to the simple but eminently practical design of the early 1960s Devon layouts, in particular the 1963 version that was in keeping with the year styling of the Fleetline. But rather than just a copy, he wanted the interior interpreted so the style was updated, using better catches and handles and modern materials.

Paul therefore contacted Tim Hartley and Vaughn Green of Custom Classic

The unit at the side of the rear seat contains a modern twin-hob cooker/grill.

and Retro, and described in fairly precise detail what he wanted, where it should be sited, and how it should look. This proved quite a puzzle for Tim to get right, because not only did he have to copy cabinet shapes and sizes, he also had to reconfigure how it all went together, as the bus was left-hand drive, which meant that everything had to swap sides; designing the cabinets behind the bulkhead proved especially tricky. In keeping with the period layout and look, Paul also specified the tra-ditional laying down of boards to make the bed arrangement (most people fit convenient and quick-to-set-up pull-out beds, or rock-and-roll beds these days), and oak cabinets faced with black laminate panels and doors.

The interior is modelled on the 1963 Devon layout with a unit containing a modern Horizon twin hob/grill and gas bottle sitting to the side of the rear seat by the load doors (with fake drawer-style facing), whilst the unit opposite, behind the bulkhead, is a toiletry cabinet (initial plans for a sink here were abandoned in favour of extra storage); on the wall facing the load doors is a Devon-style fold-down magazine rack. Two small drawers above the engine and a roof cabinet echo the Devon layout, as does the crockery cabinet on the load door; but modern-style chrome bow handles, chrome trim and a chrome pedestal table leg update the classic design. One new feature that Paul wanted was the cab door map pocket, a very useful addition. Another practical, modern

ABOVE: *Twin rear drawers faced with black laminate are another Devon styling feature.*

BELOW: *The cab door pocket, finished to match the cabinet work, is a useful addition. Interior panels have been trimmed with contrasting stitched and plain sections divided by green piping.*

update is matching oak laminate flooring to make the interior feel light and spacious. Changes in lifestyle since the 1960s are met with the subtle addition of Alpine 6 × 9 speakers under the rear bench seat, with grills cut discreetly into the base.

Whilst Tim was busy with the cabinets, Vaughn set to work on the interior trimming and the fitting of new door cards, headliner and cab carpets. The upholstery has been finished to match the exterior colours, with green piping and striping setting off the white upholstery. Stitching breaks up the cushions, and the side panels are finished with contrasting stitched and plain sections divided by green piping.

The overall feel is of old meeting new, which is exactly in keeping with the spirit of a bus built from old and new parts. In the same way that the bus looks like a Samba but has something different about its look, the interior looks and feels like a classic Devon, but a Devon with a difference. The traditional look has been retained, but updated and modernized without losing any of its period feel, and the cream vinyl and oak cabinets and flooring make for a bright, spacious and contemporary feel.

RIGHT: *The load-door cabinet has been copied from the style of cabinet used on 1963 Devon conversions.*
BELOW: *The cab seats have been trimmed to match and coordinating dark green carpets laid in the cab area and under the seats.*

purple haze
1981 Devon Moonraker

BELOW: The long side cabinet has a kitchen worktop, planed down to size, and a sink is inset into one end.

The cooker is located in the centre section of the cabinet, accessed by a hinged lid, and the cupboard is finished in matching purple.

ABOVE: The interior is finished in purple and grey, with lilac snakeskin door fronts, purple fur fabric upholstery, purple carpet and grey carpet to face all cabinets, interior panels and seat bases.

Geoff Parker bought this T25 in 2006 for the bargain price of £200! In fact the Devon interior fell apart soon after he acquired it, so he decided to rebuild his own version, on a limited budget, to his own design and tastes. The long run of cabinets under the windows, the rear wardrobe, roof locker, rock-and-roll bed and buddy-seat arrangement of the Moonraker had worked well in the space, so he decided to stick with that layout, but to give it his own interpretation.

After completely stripping the interior he then built dummy cupboards with cardboard until he had the design he was happy with, which was then tweaked after sitting in the van every day. He built up the cabinets from marine ply and covered the side unit with a piece of worktop left over from a friend's kitchen refit; as it was 2in (5cm)

ABOVE: *The circular sink was originally a dog's bowl, but proved the ideal dimensions and shape to fit into the worktop.*

RIGHT: *A fridge has not been fitted, making for extra storage space.*

ABOVE: *The elevating roof has been lined with purple carpet, and LED strips added round the vent hatch.*

BELOW: *A converted skim board, with added purple pinstriping, makes a perfect drinks table.*

thick, it needed planing down. Being an old hippy at heart with a passion for purple, Geoff decided to trim out the interior in purple shades. Soft, decadent purple fur, bought on a trip to Paris, has been used to cover the seats and bed cushions; this has a sheen to it that really sparkles and glints in sunlight. Contrasting textures and shades come from lilac snakeskin vinyl used to cover the cupboard doors, and purple carpet to reline the pop top. Light grey needlecord carpet has been used to cover the rear seat base, the buddy seat base, and all interior surfaces including cabinets, making for a softer effect. (The vinyl was sourced from Martrim of Sandbach in Cheshire, and contemporary chrome handles, as well as all catches and hinges, from Focus DIY.)

The front cab has been trimmed out to match, with purple and black vinyl panels, purple vinyl detailing in the dash, and a pair of purple and black seat covers with a Big Foot motif. Geoff has recently acquired a pair of heated,

electric Porsche seats, which he plans to have recovered in a design identical to the loose covers. A small steering wheel and a purple glass skull gear knob complete the custom look.

Geoff has a regular table for dining, mounted with a pedestal leg in the floor, but for relaxing, a customized skimboard, with added pin-striping detail in purple, makes an excellent drinks table and adds to the eclectic look.

A fridge has been dispensed with, as the old fridge had done untold rust damage, so a portable coolbox is carried instead. A twin burner/hob, with its

housing painted purple to match, has been fitted, Moonraker style, in the middle section of the side cabinet, with a longer lifting lid to access a cutlery storage section at its side. The circular sink was originally sold as a dog bowl, but was the perfect size and shape to fit the available space and has been inset into the new worktop and fitted with a multimix electric tap.

Although carpet is often thought impractical for camping, Geoff decided that laminate floor would be too cold and slippery, so a removable purple carpet has been fitted, to add to the softer feel of the interior. Finishing

ABOVE: The rear has a wardrobe and open storage areas.

ABOVE: Lilac snakeskin-pattern vinyl and contemporary steel handles are fitted to all cabinet doors. Note the roof-mounted spotlight.
LEFT: All the interior panels, roof and cabinet work, have been faced with soft grey carpet.

BELOW: *The cab door panels are trimmed in lilac and black.*

ABOVE: *Lilac vinyl has also been used to trim relief areas on the dash.*
LEFT: *A purple glass skull gear knob adds to the overall look.*

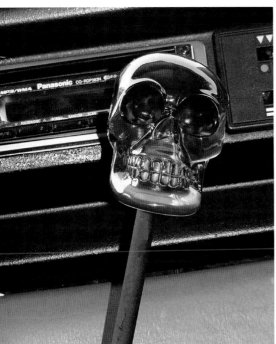

touches come from LED strip lights mounted in the pop top, flush-mounted circular lights above the long cabinet, and a moveable spot by the roof locker.

The total cost, including the bus purchase, all the interior fit-out, a new sill, 65mm lowering springs, refurbishing of the carbs, tax, MOT and insurance, came in at just under £2,000! The end result is something versatile and eye-catching that is all his own work and built to his own tastes. Understandably it always attracts attention, and is definitely *not* what people expect to see from looking at the matt black exterior! But then again, perhaps it comes as no surprise to learn that Geoff's cyberspace alter ego is the Reverend Pimp Daddy!

Future plans include a respray of the hand-painted exterior, an Oettinger body kit, changing the 16in Audi alloys for 17in versions, and getting out and about enjoying living in the 'Lurve Potion' as well as enjoying the looks on people's faces.

(Photographs courtesy of Geoff Parker)

BELOW: *A pair of funky foot seat covers, in matching colours, will soon be replaced with Porsche seats re-upholstered in the same design.*

seventies styling
1972 Swedish Camper

Robert Johnson's 1972 Swedish camper has an original, one-off 1970s interior, designed and built by its first owner; it shows how a well thought-out personal design, with its roots clearly in 1970s styling, still looks classic and distinctive.

Having removed the Microbus interior, the owner set about converting it into a camper. His day job was converting and kitting out interiors for yachts and boats, and he combined his skills and knowledge from fitting out an interior in a confined space with very clear ideas about what layouts and materials worked best. For example,

the wood is all yacht-varnished pine, and the use of curved corners on the cabinet doors, a design touch reminiscent of Westfalia, breaks up the straight lines and means no sharp edges to bang into. The layout features some unique features, including a floor-to-ceiling central cupboard, a lounging space under the side windows, and a fully self-contained demountable kitchen unit.

A three-quarter pull-out bed meets storage units that run along the side facing the load door. These are accessed from the top and used for storage, as access to the leisure battery,

ABOVE: The classic 1970s kitchen design coloured ceramic hob/sink unit harmonizes with the wood cabinets.

RIGHT: The self-contained kitchen cabinet is demountable for use outside, freeing up floor/living space when the van is camped up.

ABOVE: Water and gas bottles are stored in the base of the removable kitchen unit. Note the recessed handles to allow for easy lifting in/out.

ABOVE: A full height, two-section cabinet is fitted directly behind the driver. The hanging space has removable shelves, and a sectioned, large storage cupboard is sited under the electric fridge.

LEFT: The table is floor mounted on a pedestal leg and can be rotated to a variety of positions.

BELOW: Cabinets are finished in wood laminate, giving warm tones to the interior. Doors with rounded corners are influenced by Westfalia styling, and the grey trim and edging adds contrasting detail as well as protection.

and for a removable unit for a porta potti. Cushions lie on the top of this unit at the same height as those above the engine, to make for a lounging space. A roof unit has additional storage, and speakers and twin spots in the rear create ambient lighting. An interesting feature is the siting of a safe

under the base of the rock-and-roll bed, only accessible when the bed is made up. A chrome single-pedestal leg table is fixed to the floor, and the small rectangular tabletop can swivel to work in a variety of positions.

Opposite the load door, behind the driver, and meeting the side storage

units, is a large floor-to-ceiling unit. The rear section, with a door mirror, where a retractable television aerial is sited, can be shelved or used for hanging space, whilst an electric fridge over another shelved cupboard is sited in the front section. The zig-control panel is fitted at the top, next to which is a handy

LEFT: *Lounging space, with storage under, runs along one side under the windows to meet the rear area. The 1970s style of Scandinavian-weave fabric is a little faded, but still in good condition.*

holder for the stereo handset – meaning no more 'hunt the remote' games!

The kitchen is all contained in a demountable unit, sited behind the passenger seat by the load door. Water and gas bottles are kept in the base, and the coloured ceramic top of the unit has integral sink and twin-burner hob, the brown and cream colours of which harmonize well with the warm honey tones of the cabinets. This unit is fully removable (and even has hand recesses for easy lifting) to give maximum flexibility, and by using it in an awning, it frees up valuable living space in the bus.

Other touches include handy net-storage pockets, a dash map holder and table, and the use of contrasting grey trim on cabinet and door edges.

The original fabric is perhaps now dated in style, but a simple plain throw brightens the interior until such time as the fabric can be updated; although a roll of the original fabric came with the bus, Robert feels he wants something more modern-looking, when funds allow! In the meantime, after a muddy camping weekend, he removed the carpet and replaced it with easy to clean, wood-look vinyl flooring, sourced from a carpet retailer. The use of simple mitre edging strips brings the floor and cabinets together seamlessly.

One very luxurious touch was added by the last owner: the fitting of Porsche Recaro seats in the cab. These are shaped with lumber support, making for very comfortable long-distance travelling. The driver's seat also features

ABOVE: *The pull-out rear seat bed sits flush with the side and rear cushions to make for a huge full-width bed.*

ABOVE: *A cabinet for storing a porta potti is sited at one end of the under window units.*
RIGHT: *A safe is hidden under the rear seat base.*

A cab dash table, finished to match the cabinets, is a very useful accessory.

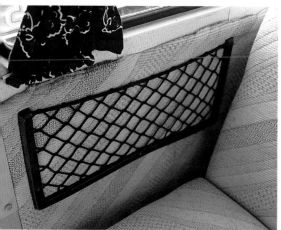

ABOVE: Net storage is a space-saving solution for books, magazines, maps and similar items.
RIGHT: Porsche Recaro seats with lumber support make for very comfortable travelling.

full electronically controlled adjustment.

The interior epitomizes classic 1970s Scandinavian design and materials, and makes excellent use of space. Whilst the layout is really suited to a couple, the addition of a child's cab bunk slung over the front seats makes for a comfy bed/rest area away from the parents, and the demountable kitchen means that living space can be greatly increased when camped up.

flower power
1966 Deluxe Microbus

ABOVE: *Cath Kidson fabric, in a design called Pop Flowers, has been used to give a retro Sixties feel, as well as add colour and brightness.*

The interior has been designed for use more as a weekender than a holiday camper, with living/sleeping space, plenty of storage, pump tap and sink and portable cooking facilities.

The headlining has been finished in the same fabric for a very different look.

Ben Whitehouse has always loved and owned classic cars, but as two-seater sports cars were not family friendly and no longer met his needs, he began to look for something classic in looks but which could also be used for weekends away at the beach.

He found the perfect solution in this 1966 Deluxe Microbus, imported from California. The paintwork was a bit faded and there were scratches and imperfections in the body, but it was basically very solid and in good order. The original Sea Blue under Cumulus White patina is partly what attracted him, as it showed signs of use and love, and the bus still had Deluxe features such as the dash clock and the bumper and beltline trim, as well as the US-spec bumpers. The classic period look has been updated with polished Empi 5s and safari windows, the motor has

ABOVE: Cab seats are finished in cream leather, with stitched pleat and Teal piping detail. The same colours are carried through on to the door panels.

LEFT: At the rear of the main unit is a storage compartment accessed from the top. The unit also provides a long run of shelf or worktop space.

been replaced by a 2.2 Scat version, and the new interior, with its bright 1960s-style Cath Kidson fabric, makes for a perfect retro modern look inside.

The original Microbus seats were removed (and stored), and Ben set about designing the interior. After much looking, he finally found a style he liked on display at Vanfest, kitted out by Neil Roberts of Custom Made Interiors in Poole. Influenced by the 1978 Devon Moonraker layout, with the kitchen and storage units running under the windows, it has been built from maple, giving a modern, light look. Neil makes bespoke furniture for houses and boats and had developed some bus furniture because of all the

interest in the interior he had built for his own Split Camper.

Ben sat down with Neil and outlined his ideas and needs, which would work around the basic layout. As the bus was a bulkhead model it was decided that a dinette style of two facing benches round a table and with storage under would be best, and because Ben wanted to keep a period feel, the bed is made up in the traditional method of laying the table between them.

The bus was not for use as a holiday camper: what Ben wanted was more of a weekender, so a built-in cooker was not needed. Instead a portable, single-burner hob is carried in the top of the unit. Ben did decide, however, that a

LEFT: A modern sink and portable camping stove are located under the lifting shelf top: ideal for days by the beach.

BELOW: Door cards are trimmed in original Microbus style, and match the upholstery.

flower power: 1966 Deluxe Microbus

RIGHT: All cabinet work is made from maple for a light, airy and modern feel, and the vinyl floor harmonizes with the interior wood and upholstery colours.

ABOVE: A large dining table, also finished in maple, attaches to the front of the kitchen unit.
RIGHT: Moonraker styling has been followed, with a long run of units under the windows for storage and kitchen.

small sink to wash cups and spoons was useful to have. With no heat exchangers he also wanted a Propex heater fitted.

The main kitchen unit provides a good-sized shelf/worktop, and the top section hinges up to reveal an inset, circular, stainless-steel sink and pump tap, and an area for storing or using the cooker. Under this is a cutlery/utensil drawer and storage cupboard, and a larger full-height cupboard where the

water and waste bottles are sited. The rear section of the unit is a deep storage compartment, accessed from the top by the rear seat. A large table, also finished in maple, fits against the front of the unit.

Ben also asked for two roof cabinets, the rear one for storage and an amp, whilst the front one contains a small drop-down television/DVD. Speakers are arranged for the full surround-sound cinema feel. Twin halogen light

fittings are also mounted on these cabinets, with the power management control panel fitted to the front one. (Neil's marine background shows in the use of a marine control panel here, which always arouses interest as it includes switches for the anchor light and bilge pump!) The rear area, covered with a base cushion, has been kept clear to maximize space and light, and also to provide a child's berth. A cab child's bunk means the family of four can sleep comfortably.

With the cabinets sorted it was time to have the interior trimmed. The sun-bleached colours of the original Aero Papyrus Deluxe interior panels set the tone, and Ben chose cream and Teal Blue to echo that, and to harmonize with the maple wood. The cab seats have been trimmed in cream leather with Teal piping, whilst the bench seats have been trimmed in matching style in vinyl, chosen as being more practical and 'wipe-clean' for a living area. The original pattern of the Deluxe's door panels has been followed, with a wide

Extra storage is in the rear roof locker. Note the stylish, rotating twin halogen light fittings.

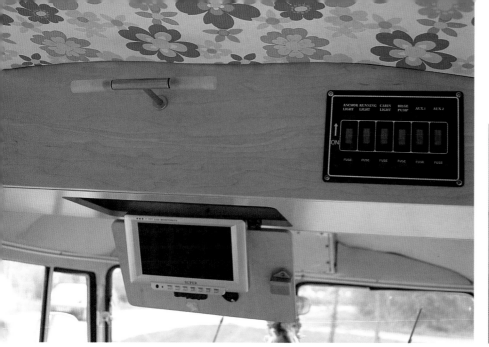

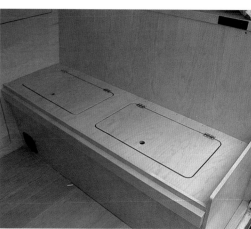

BELOW: The speakers are located in the roof locker base, and also in the front bench base. There is additional storage in both seat bases.

The stereo system and a small drop-down TV/DVD is located in a front roof locker. The control panel is a marine version, hence the switches for anchor light and bilge pump.

cream centre section flanked with top and bottom sections finished in Teal. The vinyl flooring, with creams, beiges and blues in a washed design, harmonizes with the interior colours and is also very practical.

The main upholstery and trimming was done professionally, although Ben ended up finishing off and doing the headlining himself. He chose a Cath Kidson fabric called 'Pop Flowers', because not only did it have that retro modern Sixties flower-power theme, with its vibrant and colourful design, the colours also picked up on the maple, cream and Teal used in the interior.

Sarah at VW Camper Curtains made up the curtains for him from the fabric he provided, and he also decided to go one stage further and cover the roof to match, making for a very colourful interior that you only fully appreciate when sat inside the bus. A tablecloth has also been made using the same material. Matching 'Pop Flower' pattern bedding, and a child's sleeping bag coordinate the styling, and a pair of mugs in the same Cath Kidson design adds the perfect finishing touch.

ABOVE: Coordinated bedding, curtains and crockery make for a bright, homely feel.
BELOW: The bed is laid down in the traditional way for a period, classic camper feel, whilst the rear has been kept open for light and space, as well as providing a child's berth.

poppy
1978 Panel Van

LEFT: The interior has been finished in red and white to coordinate with the exterior colours. Details such as red curtains lined in white, carpet-covered seat bases, and pine worktops, table and shelf, all add to the overall effect.

BELOW: A single bed is made up using a flip-up base on the end of the front bench seat. The bulkhead is trimmed to match the panels, and the red end cushion with white VW logo adds a personal styling detail.

This 1978 former panel van is named Poppy, for obvious reasons. When Alan Cutts acquired her, she had had side windows fitted and had been converted into a camper, with an interior that Alan describes as 'looking like it had been in Pimp My Ride!' Taking the red and white exterior colours as the theme for the interior, Alan has transformed the camper into something designed specifically round the needs of his family, and what's more, has had the satisfaction of doing all the work himself.

The makeover all started when he decided to update the front seating arrangement. Not happy with his daughter having to sit in the back with no seat belt, he acquired a belted double and single cab seat set-up, with headrests, from a Ford Transit, which would mean that all three could sit together in the front in safety. However, it was not as simple as it sounded, and fitting the seats actually involved a lot of grinding and welding and cursing! Alan also decided to reupholster the seats himself using an industrial sewing machine, and chose poppy and white Ambler vinyl to match the red and white of Poppy's exterior. The

ABOVE: *The worktop on the side units is made in polished pine to match the table top.*

ABOVE: *Sleeping for the family of three is easy, with the three-quarter rock-and-roll bed and single bulkhead bed. Note the pine shelf under the windows.*

BELOW: *A Snap On toolbox, in matching red with pine top, is located in the rear. Extra bed cushions are stored in the rear area, which is covered in carpet to match the seat bases.*

white centre panel sections have been finished with a horizontal stitch pattern, which gives a racing look to the seats. The new seats looked superb when finished, but they put the rest of the interior to shame, so Alan decided he had to rip out the camping interior and start all over again!

Once he had sorted the front seating, he sat down and sketched out what the rest of the interior might look like. As they intended using the camper a lot, the design had to be simple and practical – but he didn't want something that looked too modern or that would date quickly: he wanted a classic, timeless look that retained a

period 1970s feel for the age of the bus. The interior needed to sleep two adults and a child, and have cooking facilities. Alan also wanted to incorporate a built-in toolbox, choosing the 'Snap On' range would coordinate with the camper's colours; he was also inspired by the American Hot Rod style of clean lines, with all the panel fixings hidden.

After making a framework for the interior panels, they were covered in matching poppy and white vinyl, with the white centre sections finished in a stitched design to match the front seats. The headlining took three attempts to fit, and Alan ended up having to make a

The side unit contains a cooker/grill, and a small crockery compartment accessed from the top.

mould the same shape as the roof. He then laminated two sheets of 1.5mm ply together, and put this into the mould until it curved to shape, before covering it with the headlining cloth.

A heavyweight industrial vinyl floor has been laid down on the main floor area for easy cleaning, and TVR carpet fitted in the front and back. Matching carpet has been used to cover the seat bases. The old rock-and-roll bed was taken out, cleaned up and reused with new foam cushions, which were then reupholstered to match the cab seats and interior panels. Opposite this Alan built a useful storage box/seat that incorporates a flip-up end, which can

The side cabinet has been painted red to match the upholstery, and fitted with recessed chrome handles.

become a small single bed with the help of some screw-in legs and another cushion; the back cushion is stored in the front when not in use. The unit doubles as dinette-style seating, allowing four to sit comfortably round the table. A nice finishing detail is the white VW logo stitched into the red single end cushion.

A unit for the cooker/grill is located at the end of the rear bench seat, with a useful crockery cupboard at the rear. This was made out of 10mm and 12mm MDF, and then spray-painted red with an acrylic paint in keeping with the interior colour scheme. It has been given a worktop of French-polished pine to match the table, and matching

pine windowsills have also been fitted. Behind the cooker unit towards the back of the van is a permanently fixed red 'Snap On' toolbox, with a matching pine bench top. The open front rear roof unit, which also contains a pair of speakers, was part of the original interior, and has been re-covered in white vinyl. The look has been finished off with matching red curtains lined in white, adjustable spots in the roof, chrome cab window-winder handles, chrome recess handles on the units, and a leather steering-wheel cover.

Alan has also lowered the bus and fitted a 1641cc motor, twin Kadron forties, Thunderbird four-into-one exhaust,

and a 009 distributor. All the work has been carried out by Alan himself, though he says he could not have done it without understanding wife ('Do you really need two carburettors?'), an enthusiastic daughter and an industrial sewing machine! The end result is something Alan is rightly proud of.

Building and trimming the interior may have been a steep learning curve, but the end result of having carried out the work from design to reality himself has been deeply satisfying. The interior is clean, bright, and suits the needs of the family perfectly.

(Photographs courtesy of Alan Cutts)

LEFT: Door and interior panels are trimmed to match the seating, and all fixings have been hidden to keep clean lines.

BELOW: Work in progress!

updating a classic
1965 Westfalia SO 42 Camper

How do you improve on a classic interior design such as an early Westfalia? The simple answer is you can't, and to modify or alter it would be like rewriting history – but what you can do, as in this case, is to update the look to give a contemporary feel. By just changing the colours and interior finish you can end up with something new and distinctive that looks totally period, and yet still retains all its classic, period features.

This 1965 Westfalia SO 42 Camper had been badly abused in the past: it had ended up being hand-painted in black both inside and out, and had even had the wheel arches cut out to accommodate wide rear wheels! Despite this, all the original Westfalia interior was actually complete and intact, so new owners Simon and Emily Hunt decided that, rather than restore it to its original condition and finish, they would themselves update the look whilst trying to keep an authentic period styling.

After stripping everything out of the bus, Simon bare-metalled the whole

ABOVE: All the cabinets have been relaminated in blue-grey Formica to harmonize with the exterior; this makes for a modern, stylish look that preserves a period feel.
LEFT: The interior colour scheme of grey and white harmonizes well with the Baltic Blue/Ivory White body colours.

BELOW: The table flaps down against the side wall when not in use, and black and white floor tiles laid in a classic check pattern add to the period look.

ABOVE: White Formica has been used as a top surface for the table, and all worktops and folding shelves.

BELOW: The full-height wardrobe by the load door was a standard feature on early Westies. Grey push handles and contrasting white trim round door edges on the cabinets keep the interior colour scheme coherent.

ABOVE: The seats have been trimmed in harmonizing grey vinyl, with contrasting grey/white plaid fabric centre panels that match the curtain material.

inside by hand, using paint stripper and a scraper. The whole shell was then shot-blasted in Simon's garage prior to painting all the underneath, and prepping the body ready for its new classic colour scheme of Ivory White over Baltic Blue. The result is an exterior colour scheme that keeps the period 1960s pastel colours, and looks like an original factory combination.

They decided that the interior should carry through this colour scheme by using a blue-grey finish for the cabinets, and grey vinyl for the upholstery. A heat gun and scraper were used to painstakingly strip back the woodwork and old laminate, then all the cabinets were relaminated with smoke-grey Formica to harmonize with the exterior. Grey push-button cabinet handles are an excellent finishing detail, and all the doors have been edged with contrasting white trim, whilst white Formica has been used for the table and worktop surfaces.

Emily chose a grey and white Westy-style plaid for the curtains, and grey vinyl for the upholstery. To bring some

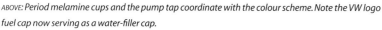

ABOVE: *Period melamine cups and the pump tap coordinate with the colour scheme. Note the VW logo fuel cap now serving as a water-filler cap.*

RIGHT: *The load door 'spice rack' unit was adopted by many other converters. Door panels also have fabric centre sections to match the curtains.*

pattern into the interior and break up the grey upholstery, the same material as the curtains has been used for insert panels in the rear and cab seats. The side panels and door panels have also been finished in matching grey vinyl with plaid inserts. Black and white floor tiles, harking back to early Devon styling,

make for a fully coordinated colour scheme inside and out. A concession to modern family life is the in-house entertainment system (fitted before the new headliner went in), which consists of a drop-down DVD, television and Play-Station 2 with headphones, conveniently sited on the air vent.

The attention to detail is everywhere in this bus: the chrome period fire extinguisher in the front cab, the grab handle that matches the grey and white colour scheme (an original Empi accessory found at a show, still in its display packaging), the whiteband tyres sourced from C & M, Wolfsburg crest

ABOVE: *The rear bed cushion matches the interior seats.*

RIGHT: *A pair of Beetle-style white bolster cushions adds a coordinated finishing touch to the rear seat.*

LEFT: The air vent is a perfect place to mount a flip-down television/DVD to keep the children amused whilst travelling.
BELOW: The two-tone grab handle also matches the colour scheme, and is a genuine Empi accessory.

seatbelts from Custom and Commercial, a Wolfsburg horn push, Blaupunkt radio, even a period chrome dash clock/thermometer.

Whilst some purists might bemoan the loss of the authentic Westy look, the end result is a subtle, understated, period-style interior that has been given a tasteful modern makeover, but which has retained all its period charm. The original cabinets and layout of the SO 42 conversion have been preserved, and to many people it looks like original styling, as the layout is exactly as it was when it left the factory; it is just the finish, materials and colours that have changed, giving a modern twist to a classic design. Now owned by Stuart Mears, it is often on display at *VW Camper and Commercial* magazine's stand at shows and a period Westfalia trailer, painted to match, hauls all the camping gear for family holidays.

RIGHT: A period chrome fire extinguisher is mounted by the driver's seat to add to the period styling.
BELOW: The plaid curtain fabric is also used for inserts in the cab seats and panels, making for a look that feels authentically stock. Note the ivy leaf etching on the window glass.

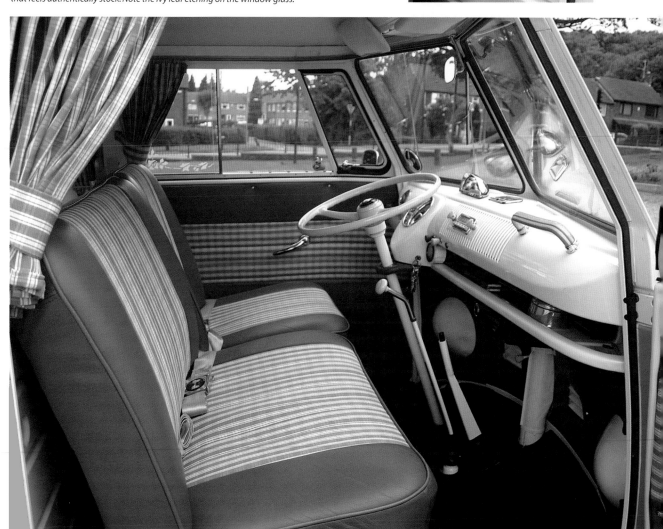

36

Dormobile with a difference
1972 Dormobile Camper

BELOW: *The main kitchen unit of Smev hob and sink, fridge and storage is finished in light carbon design Vohringer ply with dark grey trim for edges and doors adding contrast. Stainless-steel push button handles harmonize with the grey and pattern of the ply.*

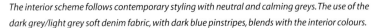

The interior scheme follows contemporary styling with neutral and calming greys. The use of the dark grey/light grey soft denim fabric, with dark blue pinstripes, blends with the interior colours.

The name 'Dormobile' is synonymous with camper vans, and it is probably one of the best known conversions, as its models were exported or built under licence all over the world. The most distinctive feature is the patent Martin Walter elevating roof, which was so successful that it was even offered as an option in the 1960s by companies such as Devon and Westfalia before they developed their own versions.

This 1972 Dormobile has retained the classic 1970s Dormobile layout, with units arranged along one side under the windows, but has been given a contemporary twist by the use of modern materials and colours, which echo the styling and look of current conversions, including VW's own T5 California.

When John and Louisa Thompson acquired the bus it was complete, but very rough. They decided to completely revamp the interior rather than refurbish it, and to update the look with something clean and modern, but which still retained the original layout concept and would sleep four in comfort. After looking round shows and searching the internet, they contacted Jon and Sue at Calypso Campers, as their bespoke service and use of modern materials offered exactly what they wanted. In particular they liked the fact

ABOVE: *Cab seats have been upholstered in grey leather with light grey centre panels to coordinate with the light/dark grey striped fabric on the rear seat. Door, kick-panel and under-seat areas are trimmed in grey.*

LEFT: *All the interior panels and roof areas are finished in grey carpet-style material for warmth and insulation as well as design continuity.*

that each Calypso interior is unique, and everything, from electrics to fittings, appliances and upholstery, is provided on site – plus, of course, the wealth of advice and ideas that come from years of providing a tailor-made service.

Initially they wanted to fit a full-width rock-and-roll bed, but when Jon pointed out that this would mean losing valuable side storage space, they decided against it, and instead opted for a three-quarter bed; they also decided to follow the original Dormobile layout, with all the units running along the side under the windows opposite the sliding door.

Behind the driver is the main kitchen unit, with separate stainless-steel modern Smev hob and sink, with a three-way fridge and storage under. Another unit, set back to give more living space, runs right through to the rear, providing top-accessed storage and front-accessed cupboards to the power management system. The rear seat base has front-accessed storage; it also has speakers and 240V/12V sockets, and the table is stored under the roof cupboard when not in use.

The Dormobile style of hanging closet/folding seat behind the passenger seat has been replaced by a larger, removable buddy seat that also contains a porta potti. Lighting is provided by a reading spotlight on the side of the roof unit and two fluorescent strips.

ABOVE: *A chrome pedestal-leg table, with sharp corners softened for safety, keeps the modern styling theme. Grey vinyl flooring adds to the coordinated interior look.*

BELOW: *The old, awkward style of Dormobile bed arrangement that used the table has been replaced with a rock-and-roll bed. The seat base has speakers and the 240V socket.*

By having only a three-quarter-width bed, space is created for storage at the side.

The conventional layout has been given a modern twist by its use of light carbon-pattern Vohringer ply trimmed with dark grey edging and rounded corners, and a chrome pedestal-leg table, making for modern styling and clean lines.

The silver-grey vinyl flooring, grey side panelling, grey roof bunks and bold stripe-pattern seat upholstery (Shades of Grey an Indian soft denim fabric) all coordinate with the cabinet-work, making for a calm, unified feel to the interior. The colour theme is carried through into the cab area, with seats trimmed by DB Cartrim in dark grey leather with pleated lighter grey leather centre panels, and door and kick panels trimmed to match the rear sidewalls and roof.

New elevating roof fabric, finished in red to match the exterior colour of the bus, was sourced from Dormobile, and all the struts and supports were refurbished in silver grey to harmonize with the rest of the interior. The large check-pattern curtains in dark red and grey also match, with the subtle use of the red bringing in colour and harmonizing with the red paintwork. Outside,

ABOVE: The Dormobile roof, with its windows, makes for a light and spacious interior.
LEFT: New cab bunks have been made up using grey fabric. Grey/dark red plaid curtains harmonize with exterior and interior colours.

the striking red colour is set off by the white roof, and the addition of Radar alloys with matching red centre caps adds a subtle custom look.

The overall result is a modern interpretation of a classic interior layout that is functional and aesthetic. Whilst closely modelled on the original Dormobile designs, touches such as the pedestal-leg table, removable buddy seat and rock-and-roll bed make better use of space, and the use of modern fabrics and subtle colours makes the whole interior light and airy, and gives a 21st-century look to traditional styling.

(Photographs courtesy of John Thompson)

open space
1967 Microbus

The first thing that everyone comments on when Steve Riley opens the side doors on his 1967 bus is how much space there seems to be inside. With furniture kept to a minimum, a large floor area is exposed, and pale beige woolcloth-lined panels take away the utilitarian look, so the interior is opened up, yet still has a cosy feeling.

The bus was originally a Microbus with a middle row of seats, and it had already been repainted and mechanically overhauled when Steve acquired it. He was after something that would enable him to enjoy his other passion – BMX biking – and his starting point was to create an interior that was comfortable enough for him to relax in at

events, but which would also allow him to carry several BMX bikes. So the basic design of rear seat, sound system, small removable table, and plenty of floor space with hard-wearing, wipe-clean flooring has been built specifically to accommodate these needs.

Steve works for a coach-building company that specializes in kitting out buses, coaches and mobile libraries, and he has been able to use the same hard-wearing, practical fabrics when trimming his own interior, as can be seen in the bright fabric for the rear and cab seats, which is normally used to upholster coach seats. One of the first jobs he carried out was to fit new headliner in a light beige vinyl, and he

ABOVE: The Pioneer head unit is discreetly contained in a unit covered in woolcloth to blend into the bulkhead; a drinks optic is sited conveniently by the load door.

RIGHT: The interior has been designed to combine maximum floor space with a cosy feel from woolcloth lining to all walls and panels. A bench seat, circular drinks table and a sound system are the only other essentials.

BELOW: The original mouldings and pressings of the bulkhead and spare-wheel well have been retained, rather than boxed in.

ABOVE: A CD storage cabinet is covered in the same soft beige woolcloth as the interior. Note the finishing details, such as the Devon trim on the panels and the oak trim topped with a chrome strip under the windows.

ABOVE: Authentic coach fabric has been used to cover cab and rear seating.

BELOW: The rear seat, complete with bus-motif scatter cushions and speakers inset into the oak kick panel, runs full width, and the interior feels spacious and roomy, with clean open lines continuing into the rear.

has carried this colour through to the interior panelling. Next came flooring, which is light grey industrial vinyl with an embossed small circle pattern to make a non-slip surface. Beige woolcloth has been used to line the door cards and interior walls, and, rather than panel in the bulkhead, the original pressings and mouldings for the spare wheel have been preserved, maximizing space and making for a workmanlike look.

The panels have been broken up with the addition of Devon table trim, which has also been used to edge the table and round the spare wheel well. The addition of check-plate metal kick corners on the cab doors, gas pedal and as footmats has been done for protection from damage by his heavy workboots. Silver detailing carries through into the cab on the steering column, pedal stalks and levers, coupled with large chrome door and grab handles. A drinks/can holder on the passenger door, and an LED lighting strip across the dash, are personal touches added for relaxation.

The main area has been kept simple. A full-width seat runs across the rear; as Steve doesn't use the bus to sleep in on a regular basis, a rock-and-roll bed would have taken up too much space.

ABOVE: A small, circular drinks/coffee table, edged with Devon trim, is floor-mounted on a single chrome leg; it is easily removable to create even more carry space.

RIGHT: Genuine transfers, as applied to buses and coaches, decorate the cab air intake vent.

Bus-motif scatter cushions add another personal touch. Mounted on the bulkhead in a woolcloth-covered casing is a Pioneer head unit that feeds Ministry of Sound speakers mounted in the seat base and a free-standing 500-watt sub-woofer. Next to this, by the load door, is a drinks optic for evening chasers. When he is with the bus, Steve spends most of his time using the sill to sit on, so the optic sited here is very convenient. This favoured sitting position has also influenced the design of the small circular drinks/coffee table, in that it is floor-mounted with a central chrome leg; its size and shape, and the fact that it can be moved out of the way easily, therefore keeps plenty of free space in the interior, whilst the height is just perfect when sitting between the load doors.

In a tribute to his favourite drink, Stella Artois, a circular Stella logo has been mounted in the centre circle of the bulkhead spare wheel pressing. A small CD rack, also covered in the beige woolcloth, is sited opposite the load doors, and there is additional storage area under the roof shelf above the engine compartment. Oak trim to match the oak seat base, topped with chrome strip, runs under the windows, and a Maltese Cross and bus decals, dash bud vase and painted dash motif, and a colourful transfer (as found on coaches) on the cab air vent are finishing touches that add more personal styling.

In keeping with the open interior theme, the rear area has been kept clean, and carries the sound system remote, toolbox, jack, and Empi motif medical kit, with a chrome rear luggage

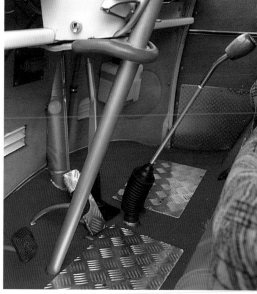

ABOVE: Details such as dash LED light strip, star motif and bud vase add personal styling detail.
LEFT: Cab doors have metal check-plate kick sections for added protection, and feature large chrome pull handles. Note the handy drinks holder for the passenger!

protection rail and check plate to face the seat back.

Steve set out to create something spacious and roomy that would maximize carrying space yet still be somewhere he felt comfortable and relaxed in, and the utilitarian feel of a load-lugging panel van or Kombi has been softened by the use of woolcloth, bright seating upholstery and personal styling details, whilst the inside has been opened up to maximize and emphasize the interior space and fit Steve's lifestyle perfectly.

RIGHT: The metal check plate theme is developed through matching floor footplates and gas pedal, with silver detailing on the steering column, pedal feet, brake and gear levers and air intake duct. The woolcloth scheme is also carried through on the cab kick-panel and headlamp mouldings.
BELOW: The rear area is also open, with the check-plate theme carried on to the seat back.

from people carrier to camper
1987 Caravelle

LEFT: Polished oak cabinets run under the window, and the mellow wood tones harmonize with fabrics, carpet and exterior paint.

BELOW: The Smev hob is offset behind the driver, and the worktop curves round to meet the run of cabinets under the window.

This T3 started life in 1987 as a seven-seater Caravelle, and was bought from its first owner by Elaine and Peter Murkin in the mid-nineties: they used it as a comfortable people carrier for several years. Then Peter retired, and with Elaine's retirement approaching, they decided that rather than buy a camper van to use in their new leisure time, it would make much more sense to convert their existing Caravelle into a comfy camper!

They started looking at interior layouts for inspiration at shows, and then came across Simon Weitz of Interior Motive. They were immediately impressed with the quality of his work and his ideas, and commissioned him to design and build the interior they had in mind. Simon prides himself on turning dreams into reality, and after discussions, produced some sketches and ideas for a layout that would be both stylish and practical. They wanted

ABOVE: *The fridge is sited under the hob, with circular ventilation holes in the cabinet door and handy net storage.*

LEFT: *A matching, smoked, glass-topped Smev sink is sited in the middle giving ample worktop space on either side.*

RIGHT: *Maximum use of storage space has been provided by divided and shelved sections.*

to be able to travel in comfort and camp up whenever they felt like it, so needed sleeping, cooking and washing facilities as well as fridge, porta potti and plenty of storage.

Once plans were finalized, Elaine and Peter set about sourcing the items they wanted Simon to build in. Separate stainless-steel Smev sink and hob top were chosen, as Elaine liked the smoked glass lids and clean looks; and the fridge was chosen for its size, not because of space available. Simon then set about building the units to fit them in. Oak veneer was decided upon as it matched the gold colour of the van well, and the classic design of kitchen units running under the window to meet a large cupboard in the rear, a three-quarter rock-and-roll bed and pedestal leg table, would form the layout. A single box unit would provide both a buddy seat and house the porta potti.

However, within this classic layout are some innovative twists, as one would expect from Interior Motive. The hob unit is mounted sideways behind the driver's seat, with the fridge under, and the worktop then narrows slightly (in a curve to keep flowing lines and

A custom-built heat shield protects the side window when cooking.

ABOVE: *The rectangular oak table has a chrome pedestal leg and can rotate to a variety of positions.*
LEFT: *All the doors are fitted with push-lock mechanisms to maintain unbroken cabinet lines and surfaces.*

ABOVE: *The large hanging space in the rear follows the shape of the van.*
RIGHT: *Additional storage in the rear is accessed by removing the rear bed cushion.*

avoid sharp edges) to run under the windows, with the sink sited half way down. This increases space in the living area and makes for a long run of usable worktop area. To keep the clean lines there are no visible handles or catches; all the cupboard doors are fitted with push-lock operation. To protect the side window, an extra fold-out heat shield has been made up; and to aid ventilation, the fridge cupboard door has a row of circular holes cut into the top. The removable buddy seat/porta potti unit has been designed to clamp securely to the floor and thus not move about when travelling.

Storage has been built into every inch of space, including a handy small

space above the leisure battery at the end of the bench seat. The seat base contains speakers and also the heater outlet. The rear side unit has sectioned shelving, and twin reading spotlights are mounted under the roof cupboard. Additional storage is provided under the side cupboard and below the rear cushion.

Bernard Newbury was brought in to add the finishing trimming touches. Peter had sourced and fitted two swivelling 'captain's seats' into the cab (and was able to use the existing seat runners), and they opted for a hard-wearing fabric for the seat upholstery, finished in fawn with a faint brown small check pattern to coordinate with the

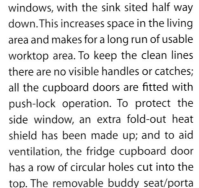

ABOVE: A three-quarter rock-and-roll bed that uses the rear area frees up space by the load door.
LEFT: The buddy seat, finished to match, has the porta potti; all clamp to the floor when travelling.

oak woodwork and gold paintwork. The door panels and headliner were still perfect and matched in, and to keep that sense of updating an original style, for the front seats Bernard made up centre panels in the same fabric, retaining the original velour side panels and vinyl base. Finishing details include removable chocolate brown carpets for cab and living area to add some warmth and harmonize with the interior colours, button cushioning on the rear seat making for a softer, living-room settee look, and two bolster cushions, finished in a gold fabric, which double as armrests or pillows.

The interior pays homage to, and updates, a classic layout, pioneered by the Devon Moonraker, but has subtly updated it to make it even more practical. Curved lines and smooth unbroken surfaces make for a modern, contemporary but classic look.

RIGHT: Swivelling cab seats have centre panels in the same fabric as the rear, but retain the original Caravelle velour side panels and vinyl base.
BELOW: The upholstery is finished in fawn with a faint brown, small check pattern to coordinate with the oak woodwork and gold paintwork. A button finish and gold bolster cushions add luxurious homely touches.

39

Kombi styling
1965 Kombi Camper

The Kombi model, with its removable middle seating and spartan interior, was designed as both load hauler and people carrier, and this Kombi Camper has taken that tradition one stage further, combining camping facilities with maximum floor space. Clean minimalist lines are combined with mild custom to make for a classic yet distinctive look.

In keeping with the Kombi concept, the bus has been finished in commercial Dove Blue and all interior exposed metal, such as dash, seat frames, bulkhead and window surrounds, are painted to match. The addition of Deluxe chrome body trim, chrome front badge, six pop-out windows, and BRM detailed wheels, add period styling and a mild custom look to what was a basic model.

The walkthrough interior has been kept plain and simple, with the focus on camping basics of rock-and-roll bed, coolbox, cooker with a grill, and a modern sound system.

ABOVE: Grey and white floor tiles laid in traditional check pattern harmonize with the panels and seats. A free-standing sub-woofer has a matching grey vinyl cover.

LEFT: All interior metal, such as the dash and seat frames, has been painted in blue to match the exterior to update the stock look. Cab seats have pleated backs and seat bases in lighter grey for contrast, and cab door panels are also finished in two shades of grey.

ABOVE: The rear seat is upholstered with a pleated stitch pattern, and beech cabinet-work with chrome fittings make for a contemporary look. A unit at the side provides additional storage and shelf top.

ABOVE: A grey steering wheel and matching gear knob, make for a unified design.

BELOW: The main cabinet contains a cooker and portable coolbox, with a storage cupboard for the gas bottle. The bracket to secure the flap-over worktop can be seen mounted on the right seat back.

Dove Blue Kombis came with a grey interior finish to seats and panels, and this stock combination has been retained and updated with light and dark grey vinyl chosen to coordinate with the Dove Blue exterior and interior paint. Instead of a plain finish, the light grey cab panels have dark grey Microbus-style centre sections, and the dark grey cab seats feature pleated light grey backs and bases. The grey upholstery and finishing details such as a steering wheel finished in matching grey harmonizes well with the Dove Blue to create an updated period look.

The modernized stock look continues into the load area, with grey and white vinyl floor tiles laid in traditional period check pattern, and combined with beech laminate for the cabinet work, to create the illusion of more space and light as well as a contemporary feel. The cargo door panels are trimmed in two shades of grey to

ABOVE: *A twin-door unit in the rear provides ample storage space. Note how the rear cushion has been shaped round the tailgate catch.*
RIGHT: *Additional speakers are mounted in a closed beech roof section.*

BELOW: *The removable coolbox is colour-coded to coordinate with the blue paintwork on interior exposed metal areas.*

match the cab door versions. The rear seat is a nearly full width rock-and-roll bed, with storage under, upholstered in pleated grey vinyl and finished with dark grey piping and chrome handles, catches and edge protection strip. At the side of this, by the load doors, is another storage unit with shelf top. More storage is provided in the rear with a two-door hanging cupboard. A closed roof section at the rear has another amp with twin flush-mounted speakers set into a beech panel.

Behind the driver is the kitchen unit, finished in beech laminate with chrome fittings; it contains the cooker/grill and a portable, colour-coded, electric coolbox. The unit's lid flaps across the gangway to make a worktop/table, and is supported in place by a hinged bracket mounted on the passenger seat bulkhead opposite. Shelved storage for the gas bottle is in a cupboard at the side of the unit, and the front section flaps down to form a useful shelf area whilst cooking. No single seat is fitted behind the passenger seat so as to maximize floor space, and a free-standing subwoofer and amp, complete with matching grey cover, travels here.

ABOVE: The interior has been designed to maximize floor and living space. Grey for interior panels and seats coordinates with the blue paintwork and echoes traditional Kombi styling.

The current owner, Toby Whittingham, has kept the interior look, apart from changing the curtains to blue/white check versions to coordinate with the colour scheme. His family of four finds the layout spacious and comfortable, with the wide rock-and-roll bed able to sleep three, and a cab bunk adding an extra child berth. The versatile layout of the Kombi has been maintained, and the use of grey in the interior keeps the traditional Kombi styling, but with a modern interpretation.

RIGHT: Dark grey centre sections to the door panels bring in a period Microbus feel.
BELOW: The top of the kitchen unit flaps across the gangway to form a worktop/table.

fun Kraftwagen
1978 Disaster Control Vehicle

The interior has been coordinated in orange and cream to match the exterior colours of the van.

BELOW: The rock-and-roll bed/rear seat has stitched cream panels and cream piping for contrasting detail.

The wide cream centre section on the sliding door panels tones down and breaks up what could be an overwhelming expanse of orange.

This 1978 Bay was one of 182 specially ordered by the German government to coordinate the work of the emergency services in case of a major national disaster or nuclear war. This one's function was to act as a *Funkraftwagen* – a radio command and control vehicle relay station – and was kitted out as a mobile office/communications centre, with generator, analogue phones, radio equipment and antenna mast, field telephones and monitoring equipment; it carried a crew of three. Built as a walkthrough panel van, it also featured the options of a single window on each side and no rear window.

Fortunately none of these vehicles ever saw use, although they were kept fully serviced and maintained, despite spending most of their time in storage. In the late 1990s they were sold off, and made excellent buys because they were still almost brand new! Graham Townsend acquired this version in 2001, and although he planned to turn it into a camper, initially he restored and fitted it out as it would originally have been for a mobile radio command centre.

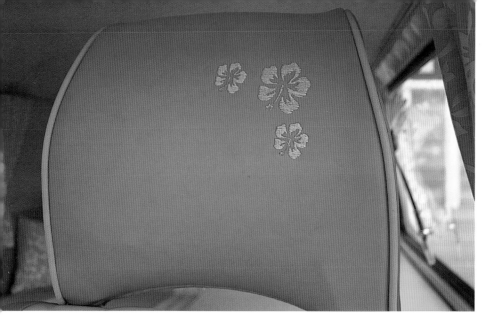

Eventually he started work on converting it into a camper, and fitted a rear window in the tailgate, a rock-and-roll bed and the wood-look flooring; he also designed and built the long side cabinet – but other things took over, and finally the bus passed into the eager hands of John Mellors and Caroline Bamford in 2007. They decided to keep the original orange colour, but to make a softer look by painting the upper half in cream, and this immediately set the styling tone for the interior colours. Graham agreed to fit the side unit he had built, and painted it in cream and orange to match the planned exterior paintwork before adding the VW motif decals to the cupboard doors.

This unit set the pattern for the interior layout and styling. Running almost full length under the side window, it offers multiple cupboard space and a long shelf/worktop area. Though the flip-top cupboard at the rear end was originally designed to take a cooker, John and Caroline wanted the interior for relaxing in: if they were out in the van, cooking could be done in an awning or, preferably, they would eat out! They do carry a portable cooker, but basically the unit with its ample cupboard spaces is used for storage. They did decide, however, to add a fold-down single buddy seat behind the driver.

John and Caroline took the bus to J & S Upholstery in Doncaster, with a basic design brief for an interior in orange and cream, continuing the theme set by the cabinet colours. This firm developed a fully coordinated

LEFT: *The cab seats have been trimmed to match.*

BELOW: *The use of cream to contrast with orange on the seat and interior panels makes for a softer, more subtle look.*

LEFT: *The base orange for scatter cushions and curtains has been chosen to match the softer orange tone of the worktop.*
BELOW: *Cab door panels are trimmed to match, and have had speakers built into them.*

RIGHT: *The spare wheel cover, in cream with orange VW logo, matches the exterior logos on the cream upper side panels. The painted generator cable access hatch frame is visible just to the right of the spare.*
BELOW: *The buddy seat frame has been finished in cream, with the white hibiscus motif embroidered on the retaining strap.*

BELOW: *A fold-down buddy seat is a perfect space-saving solution.*

look, carrying out all the trimming and upholstery, and they also made up the curtains. Matching shades of orange and cream vinyl (as used for Mustangs) were chosen for the upholstery to carry the exterior colours inside. Panels and door cards are in orange, with a wide cream centre section to break up the brightness of the orange, and the side walls are orange with cream upper sections, as in the exterior. The cream insert panels on the orange cab and rear seats are stitched for contrast, and all seat edges are finished with cream piping. The buddy seat frame is painted cream, and its seat base is also stitch-pleated.

A very personal styling touch, suggested by J & S, comes from the white hibiscus flower motif, which is embroidered on the headrests, cab seat corners, rear seat corner and buddy seat securing strap. This theme is continued in the scatter cushions and curtains, which are orange with a white hibiscus flower pattern, and with

orange gerberas in a glass bud vase on the side window. The spare wheel cover is also finished in cream, with an orange VW symbol.

The rear seat base had already been covered to match the wood-look vinyl floor: Ministry of Sound speakers are located here now, fed by a JVC head unit in the cab, with additional speakers for the cab doors. A chrome strip makes for a clean finish to the floor by the sliding door. A circular table with a pedestal chrome leg, and finished in the themed colours, is the next item on the 'to do' list!

A hint of the bus's original intended use has been preserved in the small access hatch in the rear sidewall, designed for the generator power cables; however, its frame has been painted in orange to match the other interior metal surfaces. Apart from that, the utilitarian, functional interior has been completely transformed into a bright, roomy interior that suits the needs of this family of three perfectly.

ABOVE: The wood-pattern vinyl flooring has been continued on to the rear seat base, creating the illusion of more space. Speakers have been mounted in the base.

RIGHT: The embroidered white hibiscus motif has been carried through on the scatter cushions and curtains.

Additional styling touches to the exterior include orange VW logos on side-walls and roof, chrome eyebrows and fog lights, ally side step, BRM wheels, and a three bow roofrack to complete the look.

What was once designed for a night-mare scenario has been given a new lease of life with a cheery, colour-coordinated, modern makeover, giving a whole new meaning to its designation as a 'Funkraftwagen'. Reborn, the bus made its debut at Bus Types 08, where it deservedly won 'Best Interior' in the show.

LEFT: The main cabinet features ample storage cupboards, and has been finished in cream with orange doors. Note the VW logos on each door.

BELOW: The top of the long unit makes an excellent shelf/work surface; the far end has a lift-up top to reveal storage under. Orange gerberas in the window-mounted bud vase add finishing detail.

deluxurious living room
1966 Deluxe Microbus

Deluxe Microbuses are highly sought-after models, with the roof windows and sunroof letting in sunshine and light, and chrome trim adding bling. Designed as top-of-the-range people carriers, they lend themselves perfectly to individual and custom interiors, with or without camping facilities.

This walkthrough 1966 Deluxe was imported from the USA in solid condition and still with its rows of seats. However, its new owner, Ian Bates, had something a bit different in mind! He had previously owned a 1967 original condition Devon Camper, but decided to go down the 'relax in your living room' route rather than a camping interior, as he wanted something to sit in at shows and just chill out. The only concession to traditional camper facilities was that he also wanted to be able to sleep in the bus.

Knowing already that the inside was going to be striking, the first job was to get the exterior looking right. Ian decided on a single colour, with the Deluxe's chrome trim setting it off, and went for Sea Sand, originally a 1963

ABOVE: *A Banjo steering wheel, Empi shifter and dash tachometer bring custom styling into the cab. The front kick panel is pleated to match the door and seat centre sections.*

LEFT: *Door panels and seat back have been trimmed to match the seating design and colours.*

Coordinated scatter cushions and spare wheel cover keep design unity.

Beetle colour. The bus already had Safari windows and six pop-out windows, and these, together with the door tops, were chromed to give a subtle custom look.

With the overall look sorted, Ian turned to the interior. A three-quarter rock-and-roll bed was the starting point around which the whole design took shape. In order to maximize space, and to break up angular lines and box shapes, Ian decided that the interior seating should curve so as to create flowing lines reminiscent of the front of the bus. He sketched out how this would fit under the windows and behind the driver, and then called in C + C, a local shop-fitting company, who built the unit to curve round and adapted the rock-and-roll base unit so that it would all still fit nicely in the curved space.

Speakers were fitted in the rear seat base, and under-seat storage is provided in the rest of the unit. A walnut laminate was chosen to finish the units, because it had that classic car feel, and

The seating curves round under the windows to meet the front seat, creating a roomy interior with flowing lines. Walnut laminate on the base recreates classic car looks, whilst the embossed circles on the rubber flooring maintain the circular styling theme.

ABOVE: Porsche seats have been trimmed to match with biscuit piping detail and pleated centre sections.

RIGHT: Colour-coordinated roller blinds with a retro circles pattern are fitted to the windows.

harmonized well with the pastel outside colour.

Vaughn Green was called in to trim the interior, and two-tone, off white/biscuit beige was chosen for the upholstery, to blend with the walnut interior and Sea Sand exterior, which changes in light through various shades of beige and grey. Porsche seats, trimmed in two-tone to match, a Banjo steering wheel and Empi shifter, keep the 'custom look' clean and simple in the cab, and the

two-tone pattern on the seating in the rear accentuates the flowing lines of the interior, with piping, stitching and roll edges and tops adding finishing detail. Cab and door panels and seat back panel have been finished in the same design and colours. Even the spare wheel has been covered to match, and matching scatter cushions add to the comfortable modern living-room effect.

All-weather rubber flooring, with embossed circles to echo the curves of

the interior and in a beige base colour to match the seating, was supplied by Dalsouple and is both practical and aesthetic. Roller blinds make another harmonizing touch that keeps design unity: these are finished in a retro 1960s-style fabric pattern using circles and matching colours that bring the whole interior together.

The finishing details were spotlights fitted on the roof air vent, and uplighters sited at each seat end between the

The seating, finished in biscuit and off white, has a luxurious living-room settee feel with its plain roll edges and top, piping and pleated centre sections.

window and seat; these were powered from a leisure battery and 240V inverter, supplied and fitted by Matt Grant. No living room is complete without a sound system, and a Kenwood with iPod dock feeds two 6 × 9 speakers located under the rear seat section, and two 4in speakers in the cab to give that all-important 'surround-sound' feel. By day the interior is the perfect place for simply lounging; by night it transforms into a cosy bedroom, complete with ambient lighting and chilling music.

The interior colours have been chosen to harmonize with the pastel Sea Sand exterior paintwork.

redesigning a double top
1979 Moonraker

BELOW: A Parker marine cooker, featuring a built-in oven, is located in the centre section, with an Electrolux fridge at the end.

Hinged worktop sections fold back to access the hob and sink. The original Devon sink and cooker heatshields have been retained.

ABOVE: The basic layout of units running under the window to the rear has been maintained, but has been redesigned with lots of storage space. The units are finished in birch ply.

This 1979 camper is Peter Davies' family's daily driver, covering over 10,000 miles every year. Originally built as a Moonraker, featuring Devon's new full-length elevating roof called the 'Double Top', Peter decided that it was time to create a new interior when the original 1970s chipboard began literally to fall apart. The old interior and its practical layout had served him and the family well through many years of hard use, so the starting point was to replace or redesign only what was necessary, and also to build something that offered much more storage, and which was practical for everyday use as well as holidays.

LEFT: *The unit has a worktop of pale blue Formica, bringing in a touch of colour to harmonize with the upholstery.*

BELOW: *There is additional storage in top-accessed cupboard space by the side of the rear seat; the long run of worktop provides a useful food preparation area, as well as standing or shelf space.*

ABOVE: *Drawers and box units have extension sliders, allowing them to be fully pulled out to access the whole inside area.*

BELOW: *Cushions have been re-covered in soft cotton, patterned fabric, and the rear seat has been fitted with two headrests and three inertia-reel seat belts.*

Being a kitchen designer and cabinet maker by trade, Peter was able to apply his knowledge and skills to the job. He decided to retain the basic Moonraker layout of cabinets running under the offside windows. The new units use birch ply, spray-finished in clear satin lacquer for a bright modern look with a retro 1970s feel. Birch ply is a hard-wearing material, and does not mark or dent easily, with the added advantage of not needing edging trim. All the corners are rounded off, meaning no sharp edges, and Hafele fittings and push-button handles were chosen, as he has found them to be practical and durable in the kitchen building trade.

The original Devon sink unit has been refitted at one end, under which is a new Electrolux fridge. Peter wanted to improve on the basic cooking facilities

ABOVE: A new table has been made from
matching blue Formica, but the original Devon
leg and fittings have been reused.

BELOW: A fixed buddy seat has been built around
the Eberspächer heater bolted to the floor.

A four-section unit in the rear provides yet more storage, ideal for bedding or bulky items.

BELOW: The single seat has additional pull-out
drawers and storage boxes.

and found a Parker marine oven designed for narrowboats, with a gas oven, grill and two-burner hob, which fitted perfectly into the space vacated by the old cooker. This dimension was important, as the original Devon heat shields have been reused.

The enormous amount of storage in the main unit is entirely in drawers, which means no more poking around in dark, inaccessible cupboards. Running to the rear, by the side of the rear seat, is more storage, accessed from hinged tops. These, along with the tops for the cooker and sink, are faced in pale blue Formica, which is extremely tough and adds a hint of colour to the interior. When the kitchen isn't in use, the tops fold down to provide a long, uninterrupted work surface. In the rear is a four-sectioned cupboard unit for bedding and sleeping bags, with interior shelf bases sloping back to keep things away from the doors, and an overhead locker closely modelled on the original.

The original buddy seat and the wardrobe have been replaced by a new, fixed box seat designed around the floor-mounted Eberspächer heater,

A bright contemporary look has been achieved by mixing original fittings with modern items and new materials and fittings.

with air inlets and outlets, and yet more drawers. The heater has a programmer mounted above the sliding door, which can be set to make the van as warm as toast, ready for when you wake up!

The original rock-and-roll bed has been retained and, along with the rear bed and single seat cushions, has been reupholstered in soft, dark blue, deep-buttoned fabric sourced from the Fiamma catalogue, and fitted with head restraints and inertia-reel belts for three passengers. New cab seats were from Reimo, and fitted straight on to the original seat bases. The original curtains, lino, door and interior panel lining have not been changed: they were all still in good condition, and this also means

that a good deal of the camper's heritage and feel has been retained. Likewise, although the table top has been remade in ply and blue Formica to match the worktops, the original Devon leg and fittings have been kept in use.

Additions such as speakers and the reading light in the roof locker base, 240V sockets in the seat base and on the pelmet above the worktop, and a handy kitchen roll dispenser above the fridge, all add to the practical usability of the camper. The addition of a Fiamma side awning over the sliding door gives perfect shelter from both the sun on long Continental trips and, perhaps more frequently in England, the rain.

ABOVE: The original curtains have not been changed. A handy kitchen-roll dispenser and 240V sockets have been placed above the kitchen unit.

BELOW: Speakers are located in the roof locker, and more storage space is available on top of the rear cabinet.

retro styling
1973 Westfalia

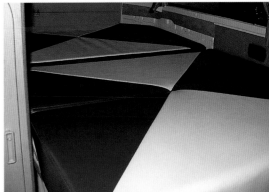

ABOVE: A V-shape pattern has been chosen for the seating to echo the old shape of the classic Splitty front. When the bed is laid out, the V lines match perfectly.

LEFT: The interior has been finished in blue and white to coordinate with the new exterior colours, and furniture remade in maple for a light, modern look.

Many interiors take as their starting point the exterior colours of the bus, creating a unified theme that harmonizes and complements these. Having repainted his 1973 Westfalia in Biscay Blue and Pearl White, David Bond from Wisconsin, USA decided this would be the basis for the interior colour scheme and updated interior styling. The original Miami interior was brown with

dark laminate cabinet work, and was quite basic, with single seat and sink/coolbox unit, fold-down table, bench seat/pull-out bed, wardrobe and rear linen cupboard. David had no intention of adding to the layout because it served his family needs perfectly, as they also tow a 1972 Eriba Puck for washing and cooking facilities when camping; what he wanted was to

modernize and update the look to create something classic that had a modern twist on retro styling. He had always loved the V-shaped front of the Split Bus models, and wanted to incorporate that idea without having to paint it on to the front panel; so he decided to carry through the V-shaped pattern on to the upholstery, which has been finished in blue and white vinyl to

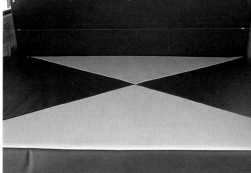

ABOVE: The cab seats have been re-covered to match, and both these and the single seat have white piping to the edges for contrast. A neat touch is the VW logos on each cab seat.

match the exterior. The upholstery was done by Erickson's Auto Trim in Menasha, WI, from shapes designed by David – and when the bed is laid out, the V lines match perfectly. The cab seats have been re-covered to match, and both these and the single seat have white piping to the edges for contrast, and the V motif stitched on to the base cushions. All the fasteners are stainless steel, adding to the contemporary look, and a neat touch is the VW logos on each cab seat.

To lighten the inside and pay homage to early Westfalia campers, maple wood has been used throughout the interior. The side panels have been lined with maple ply, and the roof lined with 3mm

ABOVE: The cab and single-seat base cushions carry through the V-motif in a stitched pattern, and blue and white matching scatter cushions add finishing detail.

BELOW: The V-pattern makes for a very distinctive interior look.

ABOVE: All the interior cabinets were templated and then rebuilt in maple to give a contemporary and airy feel. Original catches have been retained.

LEFT: Curtains are finished in the same blue and white stripe fabric as the scatter cushions, to keep the design unified.

flexible maple panelling, making for a cosy, retro look. All the interior cabinets were templated and then rebuilt in maple to give a contemporary and airy feel. To create more space, David has replaced the sink/coolbox unit with a new, smaller cabinet. The small, flap-shelf unit that was located on the side of the original unit has been used to make the top of the new cabinet, which is perfect for storing plates and utensils; and the original Westfalia cupboard latch has also been retained. As this cabinet is smaller than the original sink/coolbox,

the interior now is more spacious and roomy.

The whole family were involved in the project, and daughter Alaina even chose the floor tiles to keep the colour theme consistent. David had always liked the retro look of vinyl tiles laid in check pattern, and the blue and white tiling lifts and unifies the whole interior design, giving a modern take on a traditional style.

The pop-top canvas has been replaced, and the upper bunks and child's cab cot bunk have also been redone to

LEFT: To create more space, the sink/coolbox unit has been replaced with a smaller cabinet. The original flap shelf has been used to make the opening top.

BELOW: The period dash shelf makes for handy storage in the cab.

ABOVE: The table that folds down against the side wall has been retained, and the new cabinet opens up interior space.

RIGHT: The side walls have been lined in maple ply, in the style of early Westfalias.

match. In keeping with modern technology, a discreetly sited 800-watt custom stereo with sub-woofer and iPod dock have also been added. A model bus, finished to match the Westy, sits proudly on the dash, whilst an old German fire extinguisher (still working) adds to the period feel. Striped curtains in coordinating blue and white, and matching scatter cushions, made by David's mum Aldene, add to the finishing detail.

Whilst retaining the concept of the original Westfalia Miami layout, the end result is a modern interpretation that draws on 1960s styling, but which also has a classic yet contemporary feel. **(Photographs courtesy of David Bond)**

LEFT: Matching blue and white floor tiles make for a coordinated colour scheme.

BELOW: Flexible maple ply has been used to line the roof, adding to that vintage Westfalia look.

183

deluxe camping
1962 Microbus

This non-sunroof Deluxe Microbus was built in 1962, so still features those desirable rear corner windows, phased out in 1963. From the outset, owner Graham Dean decided to build a bus to suit his own needs, rather than restoring it to stock, and he opted for the classic pre-1958 colour scheme Chestnut Brown over Sealing Wax Red with a 2.6 T4 performance engine. It was originally a Microbus with two rows of seats, but Graham wanted to build a bespoke camping interior to his own design that had both space and room to stand or move around the table or bed.

The starting point was to have a rock-and-roll bed with units down one side under the windows and across the bulkhead, which would use curved flowing lines instead of squared angles. With a three-quarter rock-and-roll bed in place, he initially tried to draw out designs – but he quickly found the best solution was to work *in situ* using masking tape and chalk to mark up how things might fit. He wanted to ensure that all the cupboards would still open when the table or bed was in place (something easily overlooked in planning a design), and to maximize the table size to fit this.

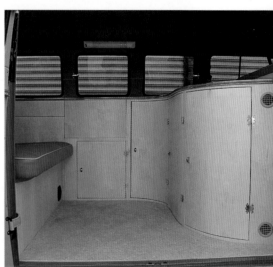

ABOVE: The interior is finished in Canadian maple with chrome push handles and butterfly hinges.
LEFT: The curving bulkhead cabinet creates modern flowing lines and a sense of space.

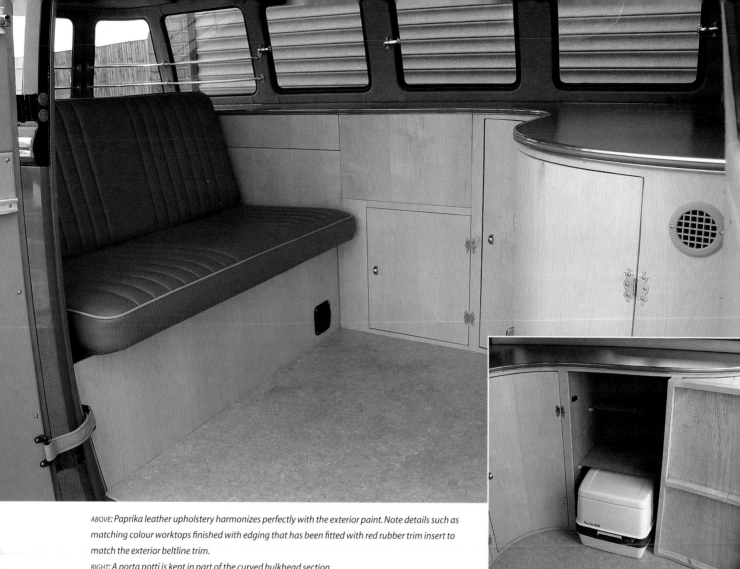

ABOVE: Paprika leather upholstery harmonizes perfectly with the exterior paint. Note details such as matching colour worktops finished with edging that has been fitted with red rubber trim insert to match the exterior beltline trim.

RIGHT: A porta potti is kept in part of the curved bulkhead section.

With the design sorted, he then built the frame from pine and ply, which he faced with Canadian maple for a light, contemporary look. The curved door fronts were achieved using 'bendy ply' (from a timber merchant), and the worktops are Solid Red Formica, a close match to the Sealing Wax Red exterior paint and sourced in a local builder's merchants. The worktops and table have been edged with Devon-style trim, which Graham has fitted with Sealing Wax Red Deluxe plastic trim insert, matching perfectly the exterior beltline trim that is standard on Deluxe buses.

Attention to details like this really make the interior distinctive and,

ABOVE: An electric coolbox is located in the unit behind the driver.

LEFT: Hinged sections, with self-locking clamps, lift to reveal the cooker and sink.

Period and original features sit side by side in the cab with modern refinements such as gauges and a CD system. Interior panels are finished in fawn vinyl, and exposed metal areas painted in the exterior Sealing Wax Red scheme. The gear lever even has a matching red leather boot.

ABOVE: The stainless-steel cooker/grill and sink unit are discreetly located under the windows.
BELOW: The sink is conveniently located at the end of the rear seat for ease of use.

coupled with luxurious Paprika leather for the seat cushions, the interior harmonizes perfectly with the exterior paintwork, keeping a period feel whilst benefiting from modern styling. The upholstery has been padded for extra comfort, and finished with a stitch pattern and fawn piping for the edges. Fawn woolcloth has been used for the headlining, keeping the period feel, and interior panels covered in fawn vinyl to resemble earlier bus interiors.

The front bulkhead unit contains the gas bottles and porta potti, as well as giving plenty of storage. An electric coolbox is located just behind the driver, and next to this is the cooker and grill (a Tasman 2500 supplied by Leisure Products Ltd, Bolton) and a matching stainless-steel sink/drainer. The unit continues through to the rear, giving more storage space. The cooker, sink and coolbox are all accessed by flapping up the worktop sections, and

BELOW: A three-quarter rock-and-roll bed maximizes interior space.

ABOVE: Red Formica worktops match the table and harmonize with the upholstery.

LEFT: The table, with edging trim to match the worktops, is mounted on the rear load door and is shaped to maximize space and access.

are fitted with self-retaining clamps to hold them in place.

The table has been mounted on to the rear load door, shaped to maximize interior space, and is also topped in red Formica with matching red insert trim. A second retaining strip on the door means the table can be positioned for outside use. Being a car trimmer by trade meant Graham had all the necessary skills and the right tools to do the job, and the interior has successfully combined his personal needs and contemporary styling whilst retaining a period feel. The curving unit draws you in, soft leather adds a touch of class and luxury, and the use of maple makes for a light, spacious feel to the interior. This is camping *de luxe* style.

BELOW: The table can also be mounted lower on the door for outside use.

funplace2b - the fun place to be
1988 Double Door Camper

ABOVE: The table stores at the side of the sink unit when travelling.

LEFT: Speaker, gas alarm and 240V sockets are mounted on the seat base, and the table leg is also clipped in place here so it is always to hand.

Double door buses were never the favoured choice of conversion companies, as having load doors on both sides means the loss of the space under the windows that is ideal for any combination of cabinets or units. However, having access on either side opens a whole new range of possibilities.

This 1988 Double Door originally had a fixed roof, but that was one of the first things new owners Alex and Kathy Fenton decided to change. It also had

an extremely basic DIY interior featuring bulkhead, an unsafe bed arrangement and a broken three-way fridge. They had the bus repainted in Poseidon Blue, and a high top roof fitted by Timber Technicians of Sherwood Forest, and for the first year they made do with a DIY interior they had designed and built themselves. However, the arrival of a new baby spurred them on to start again, creating more space and storage and radically redesigning the

whole look. Alex and Kathy are ardent all-year-round campers (they run the 'funplace2b' website, which has details of campsites worth checking out), and as baby would soon be joining them the design needed to take account of this.

Having scoured magazines and books, used VW forums, and looked at many bus interiors for inspiration, ideas began to take shape. It was important to maintain the use of both sliding

Porsche seats add luxury, and a swivelling passenger seat makes for maximum flexibility in the use of space.

doors, as the arrangement was perfect for keeping the inside cool, and also meant you could park on either side of the road and always open a slider to the pavement. To create more room and flexibility they decided to remove the bulkhead to create a walk-through, install a proper rock-n-roll bed, include a portaloo, and increase storage. An electric coolbox meant that a fridge could be dispensed with. The cooker would need a shield for protection against the wind (important with a twin slider model) and they wanted to incorporate some feature lighting. Lastly the units had to be removable for versatility.

They drafted up many drawings with a view to doing it themselves, but eventually they opted to have the work done professionally and decided to take the bus back to Timber Technicians. Steve at Gasure removed the bulkhead and fitted a pair of Porsche 911 electric seats, which necessitated the making of a new frame to fit a swivel base for the passenger seat. Timber Technicians then set about building the interior to Alex and Kathy's specifications, suggesting improvements as the build took shape. Wood laminate flooring was chosen because it is hardwearing and easy to clean, and all the interior was constructed from birch ply using beech Formica on the sides, and blue-/grey-speckled pattern Formica (to harmonize with the exterior colour) for the table, worktops and doors.

A free-standing kitchen unit with cooker and crockery/utensils storage sits behind the driver. Kathy sourced an old cooker/grill with the original windshield out of a Devon Bay, as the practical folding design maintains a classy

ABOVE: A hinge-top sink and larder cupboard are sited at the end of the rear seat, and set off with a T4 VW chrome badge.
LEFT: Double doors let in light and air, and the beech laminate flooring matches the Formica cabinet sides.

189

period feel that the modern glass-topped Smev hobs lack; and because the unit is demountable, it means that space can be freed up when camping by using it in the awning. A bracket folds out from the side to support the cooker top, which flaps across the gangway to make a useful worktop/table. Opposite this is the porta potti in a small box unit.

Next to the Bluebird rock-and-roll bed/rear seat is another storage unit with the sink and tap under a hinged worktop, with a further hinged worktop section, with storage under, running to the rear to meet the wardrobe unit. The sink unit is another salvaged Devon piece, with the pump tap updated to an electric version, and a nice touch is the T4 VW badge mounted on the end by the load door. A roof unit in the rear adds additional storage space

with more storage under the rear seat, which is where speakers and leisure battery are also sited. There are 240V sockets with stainless-steel covers fitted in the seat base, with additional sockets by the side unit mounted on the wardrobe side.

To maximize floor space a pedestal-leg circular table is mounted in the floor, and it can also be stood outside by using a Fiamma tripod base, sourced from Just Kampers. For travelling, the table clips to the side of the rear sink unit and the leg clips to the bottom of the seat base, so it is always handy! When the porta potti unit is removed (or slid under the bed) and the bed made up, there is just enough space to stand a baby travel cot, which has proved ideal for family camping. And to protect baby Summer from sharp edges

ABOVE: The cooker, sourced from a scrap Devon, has the original Devon wind/heatshield so necessary with a double door camper. The top hinges over and can be fixed across the gangway for additional work/table-top area.
LEFT: The floor-mounted small circular table brings a modern styling touch with its Formica top, and birch edging to match the cabinets, and a pedestal chrome leg.
FAR LEFT: The sink unit is also original Devon equipment, but has been updated with an electric pump tap. The side cabinet also doubles as a handy side table/shelf/worktop.

ABOVE: The table can be used outside by mounting it in a Fiamma tripod base.
LEFT: Everything can be reached easily, as the table's design and size makes for ease of movement inside.

or sticking out handles, all the doors are fitted with push-lock operation.

Still with safety in mind, a carbon monoxide detector and gas and smoke alarms have been fitted, and for warmth and insulation the roof, side walls and panels have been covered in dark beige carpet lining. Light blue curtains lined in dark blue coordinate with the overall colour scheme. The bench seat/bed is currently finished in charcoal grey, but at some point Alex and Kathy would like to reupholster it to blend with the greeny grey of the Porsche seats.

The custom ambient lighting they wanted has been achieved by the fitting of two LED strips (one blue and one in green) and four white LED spots in the roof, which give a funky wine-bar feel when Alex and Kathy settle down for the evening. The addition of a Fiamma wind-out awning adds flexibility and space, especially if friends or family pop by for a drink.

The interior layout works perfectly with the twin sliding door set-up, and having demountable units means that baby Summer can sleep peacefully in her cot whilst mum and dad cook their evening meal or sit and relax. The swivel seat and circular table add flexibility and maximize space, and the contemporary styling of the units is exactly the 'old meets new' look they were after. Funplace2b sums up what life with this camper is all about.

(And if you are looking for a VW bus-friendly campsite, check out Alex and Kathy's website www.funplace2b.co.uk /camp for a listing of sites they and friends have stayed at and recommend!)
(Photographs courtesy of Alex Fenton)

RIGHT: The side cabinet runs cleanly to meet a rear storage/wardrobe section and roof locker. Blue-grey curtains with a navy broken-check pattern harmonize with the Formica tops.
BELOW: The interior was also designed to build in space for a colour-coordinated travel cot, and the box seat slides under the bed.

renaissance fayre
1964 Panel Van

BELOW: Velvet-flocked material in charcoal grey, beige and gold swirl patterning has been used to cover the side walls, door panels, the seat base and the rear seat centre section to recreate the feel of Renaissance brocades. Sheepskin throws and rugs add a decadent touch.

ABOVE: The curved bulkhead unit maximizes access and space, and is topped in grey leather to match the cab and rear seat sides, and to coordinate with the exterior grey paintwork. A grey Venetian blind continues this colour unity and brings in contemporary styling.

Clive Miles' panel van interior is rooted in the Renaissance movement's iconography and art, but represents a diverse blend of styles and artistic movements. Having seen Joseph Beuys' installation *The Pack* in the Tate Modern, Clive was inspired to create an artistic statement that celebrated the timeless quality of objects, based around the enduring VW bus. Beuys' installation has twenty-four sledges laden with survival gear tumbling from the back of a VW Kombi; Clive has created his own artistic statement that brings together an eclectic mix of Renaissance and modern styling. His aim was to have a mobile art form that could travel to cities and act as a showcase for artists to bring their work to the general public. These travels and exhibitions would be recorded both in moving images and in print.

His starting point was the local 1930s cinema in the sleepy town of Coleford in the Forest of Dean: the cinema has remained virtually unchanged over time, with its Art Deco architecture and fittings. He also had the idea of recreating an Edwardian Gentleman's Club, with its leather settees, flock wallpaper and silver platters and candelabras. Initially he planned to show moving images projected on a screen mounted on the bulkhead in the bus, and serve cream teas and strawberries to recreate that sense of a time gone by – but he soon realized that an awning would be a much better place to site a projector and large screen.

The interior has been designed around the shape of the van. By day it's a plush sitting room, by night a

BELOW: The rear area is used to display a variety of classic objects from a blue/white china picnic set to novels by D.H. Lawrence. Note the enclosed front section of the roof that contains the ICE head units.

BELOW: A unit mounted on the rear load door, and covered in the same velvet flock fabric, flaps down to form a display shelf resembling a silver salver.

ABOVE: Both load doors are used to display an eclectic mix of classic design artefacts.

boudoir, with general living all in an awning. Modern technology in the form of LED lighting, flatscreen television, PlayStation and 1,000W JBL amps and sub-woofers, is discreetly hidden from view, allowing the interior to reflect a diverse mix of artistic influences.

Velvet-flocked material in charcoal grey, beige and gold swirl patterning has been used to cover side walls, door panels, the seat base and the rear seat centre section, recreating the Italian brocades developed in the 1600s and echoing the William Morris Art and Craft movement of the late 1800s, which came back into fashion in the 1920s and 1930s (especially in theatres, music halls and cinemas). This sets the tone for the rest of the interior, with gilt-framed Renaissance-style paintings, gold cherubims and a carved dark

oak-framed oval mirror hung on the wall. The religious influence of the seventeenth-century Italian painters is found in the triptych and framed portraits of Madonna and child, Michelangelo-style sculpture and the painted crucifix mounted in the dash bud vase.

A grey leather bench seat from a Jaguar (a modern classic) has been fitted in the cab, and a full-length grey hide, sourced from a friend who works for Landrover, has been used to trim the rear seat sides and bulkhead cabinet top. The rest of the bulkhead cabinet, with a curved cocktail cabinet-style

CONFERENCE ROOM 1

ABOVE: The front load door has a brass 'Conference Room' plaque, gilt-framed wedding photo, feather boa and Clive's favourite hat.

RIGHT: The rear load door displays include a vintage ice bucket, cake stand and storage jar and a modern clock.

BELOW: The bulkhead unit is faced with light grey fabric and features a sunrise motif. The top acts as a display shelf for flowers, paintings, sculptures, silver coasters and Renaissance-influenced religious objects.

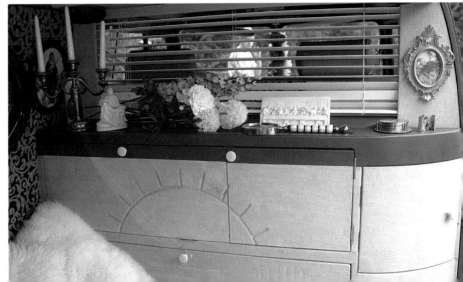

renaissance fayre: 1964 Panel Van

RIGHT: *Modern technology such as a television/PlayStation monitor is discreetly hidden away in the bulkhead unit.*

ABOVE: *Ornate-framed landscape pictures and a wood tryptich depicting the Madonna and child add to the Renaissance theme.*

RIGHT: *Scatter cushions with a classic Indian embroidery and elephant design bring in elements of Eastern styling to the mix.*

end, has been covered with grey cotton fabric and features a sunrise motif in the centre. This cabinet contains the television/PlayStation monitor and the amps for the sound system, and in a matching roof unit above this are the head units that power these. A grey slatted Venetian blind dividing the cab and living areas brings in a modern styling touch to this eclectic mix.

The rear load door has a small unit with flap-down door shelf, covered in the same flock fabric as the interior panels. The inside of this door is faced with polished steel to resemble a silver salver when open, on which stands an ice bucket, a 1930s-style cake stand and storage barrel, and a silver hip flask for that Gentleman's Club feel. A polished steel-framed circular clock is in keeping with the silver theme, adding a contemporary touch. The front load door has an authentic brass 'Conference Room' plate, Clive's wedding picture in an oval gilt frame, and a feather boa that reminds us of the roaring twenties.

JBL 1,000W speakers and amp are located in the base of the bulkhead cabinet.

ABOVE: *The rich velvet flock walls, with gold detailing and swirling patterns, have gilt-framed paintings and cherubims to add to the Renaissance art theme.*

LEFT: *Classical religious iconography is represented by pictures of the Madonna, a glass vase with a painted figure of a blessing Jesus, ornate candelabra and Renaissance-style sculptures.*

The mix of artistic styles and influences is also seen in the rear, with a classic blue/white china picnic set, chrome electric fan, and books such as *Classic Cars of the Sixties* sitting beside novels by D.H. Lawrence and works by the Romantic poets. Sheepskin throws, a rug and large scatter cushions add a touch of opulence, whilst another pair of cushions with a classic Indian elephant motif brings in an Eastern influence that also harks back to the Raj.

The whole look celebrates classical influences and period artistic styles in a way that pays homage to an enduring, rich and varied cultural heritage. Classical religious iconography sits next to modern technology in a way that startles and provokes – which is what Art is all about. No one can look at this bus and not have an opinion, and ultimately, it is the expression of individuality. Clive plans one day to take the bus to Italy, the birthplace of the Renaissance movement, and a personal vision influenced by the Sistine Chapel roof may then add to the eclectic mix of style and form.

RIGHT: *A luxurious leather cab bench seat was sourced from a classic motoring icon – a Jaguar.*

BELOW: *The religious theme is continued in cab detailing of a painted crucifix, whilst a seven pool-ball gear-knob brings in 1960s custom styling.*

195

silver dream machine
1999 Panel Van

ABOVE: The rectangular swivel-mounted table can be arranged in a variety of positions, including facing the swivel passenger seat.

BELOW: The cab seats and lounge seat have been upholstered in Pyra Grey cloth. Miami Blue piping around the seats and headrests finishes the look, and an additional personal touch can be seen in the stitched blue surfboard Calypso logos.

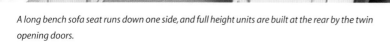

A long bench sofa seat runs down one side, and full height units are built at the rear by the twin opening doors.

Calypso Campers are well known for their bespoke one-off designs. This sleek silver machine actually started life in 1999 as a humble panel van, but it has now been transformed into something very special and stylish. It was acquired by Jon and Sue of Calypso Campers to convert for their own use at shows and for holidays. As it was to be their own vehicle, they decided a two-berth conversion would be enough for their needs, but as it would also showcase and promote their business, they chose to create a very different style of interior layout, which would be both striking and practical.

Because this T4 model has rear double doors as well as the side sliding door, John decided to have a central gangway with units on the sides and to site a fold-out bed along one side instead of using a bench rock-and-roll

ABOVE: Walnut facing on the dash is a luxury classic car touch, and contrasted with a modern custom Momo steering wheel.

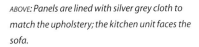

ABOVE: Panels are lined with silver grey cloth to match the upholstery; the kitchen unit faces the sofa.

RIGHT: A modern glass-topped Smev combination drainer/hob and sink brings in innovative design styling for small interiors, saving space where space is at a premium.

seat. This layout would also enable access all the way from the rear doors through to the cab.

A bench-style sofa seat runs down the side opposite the sliding door, with end bolsters to give the feel of a settee with armrests. This folds out on legs to form a huge 6 × 4ft (2 × 1m) bed, and it can also be partially laid out to use just half of it for relaxing. At the end of this is a unit for crockery and utensils, with a worktop area that also features a very useful slide-out extension leaf and a handy 240V socket – perfect for the kettle or toaster. In the roof above is a unit with an open-front storage shelf and the power management control

panel, with downlighters set in its base.

Running from the sliding door to the rear is the kitchen area, comprising a space-saving combined Smev stainless-steel hob and circular sink over cupboard space (which also contains the water container and gas bottle), and a floor-to-ceiling unit behind, by the rear door, for the fridge and more cupboard space. Above the hob is an open-fronted storage shelf unit, under which is another downlighter to illuminate the cooking/washing area.

An adjustable swivel table is mounted on the seat base behind the driver, allowing for dining using the swivelling cab seat and the lounge seat; lighting is

BELOW: The rear unit at the end of the sofa is perfect for crockery and kitchen utensils, with a slide-out additional worktop/table. A handy 240V socket makes this an ideal place to boil a kettle or make toast.

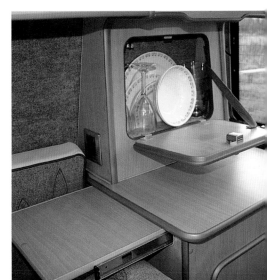

ABOVE: The fridge has been thoughtfully mounted above floor height in the kitchen unit, helping to prevent backache.

LEFT: Greys and blues harmonize with the beech finish for a contemporary and stylish understated look.

provided by six spot and strip lights. A feature that can only be appreciated at night is the siting of blue neons in the base of the bench seat to create a warm, cosy feeling when settling down for the evening. Colour coordinated custom speaker fronts sit discreetly on either side of the van side walls, and there are additional 240V/12V sockets on the unit by the sliding door.

Silvers and greys with blue detailing are the base interior colours, chosen to coordinate with the exterior. Colour

has been brought in by finishing the cabinets in beech Vohringer ply for a light, modern look, with contrasting silver trim for edges and door surrounds. The thought that has gone into the design is epitomized by the way the unit by the door features curving edges at the access point, meaning no sharp corners to catch yourself on when climbing in or out of the vehicle, and by the way the fridge has been mounted above floor height for easier access with less bending. The cab seats

and lounge cushions have been upholstered in Pyra Grey cloth, with Evolve grey vinyl for the sides. Miami Blue piping around the cushions, bolsters, seats and headrests finishes the look, and an additional personal touch can be seen in the stitched blue surfboard Calypso logos. Silver-grey cloth headliner and panelling harmonize with the interior upholstery colours, as well as adding warmth and soundproofing, and light grey check plate-pattern vinyl flooring is both practical and aesthetic. Dark

The cabinets have all been finished in beech Vohringer ply for a light, airy look with silver trim for edges and door surrounds to provide contrast detail. Light grey check plate-pattern vinyl flooring ties in with the greys and silvers of the interior.

ABOVE: The galley design maximizes the use of interior space and enables easy access from side and rear.

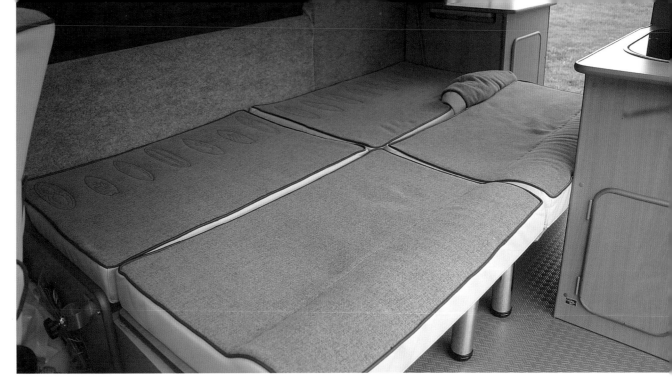

ABOVE: *The sofa pulls out to form a large 6 x 4ft double bed.*

LEFT: *A roof unit at the rear contains the power management system and provides more storage. Downlighters in the base give ambient lighting. Note the colour-coordinated custom speaker outlet mounted on the side wall.*

blue pleated blinds are fitted to the side and rear windows, making for complete privacy.

As well as a totally transformed interior, the exterior of the van has also had a complete makeover. BMW Silver over Audi Silver Grey with blue Calypso decals make for a striking colour combination that echoes the interior colours, whilst the addition of custom body touches – such as R32 Golf alloy wheels, Project Zwo twin headlights and grill, electric windows and colour-coded mirrors, three sunroofs, tinted side windows and colour-coded big bumpers – make for a mean street look. The space created by having a walk-through layout from the rear, with units at either side, makes many people think it is actually a long wheel-base model – and the number plate T4 COOL says it all, really!

ABOVE: *Blue pleated blinds that discreetly fold away make another coordinating and very modern design touch.*

LEFT: *The interior has been designed for two people to camp in style and comfort: the layout draws you in and round, giving a sense of space, and calming greys and blues harmonize with the exterior colour scheme. The cabinet corners have been rounded off and curved for safety.*

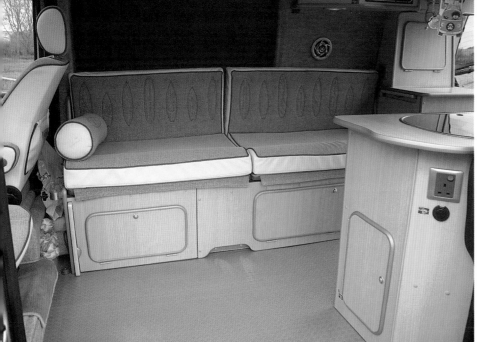

stylish samba
1966 Deluxe Microbus

After holidaying with friends in California and driving round in their beaten-up Samba, Jimi Woolley had become hooked on VW buses and knew he had to have one. In the autumn of 2003 he spotted this 1966 Deluxe on eBay, and moved quickly to close the deal. It had been imported to Houston where it had spent all its life, and although clearly in need of work, it still had all its original accessories including chrome trim, jail bars, Safari windows, Sapphire radio, dash clock, whitewall tyres and even an original Westfalia roofrack.

When it finally arrived in the UK, however, Jimi began to realize the extent of the work needed; it had sat outside without its sunroof and skylight windows and all the rear floor areas now needed replacing! After having it sand blasted to bare metal and some panels replaced, he decided to repaint it in its original colours of Titian Red under Beige Grey, keeping the outside as original and stock as possible. The inside is a different matter however, and the bus has been transformed from people carrier to luxurious living room that makes the most of internal space.

BELOW: Seating has been arranged in an L-shape to maximize space.

Alcantara faux suede and grey vinyl are colour-matched to the Titian Red/Beige Grey exterior paint colours.

ABOVE: Centre sections of interior panels have been finished in soft Alcantara, featuring a distinctive stitched diamond pattern.

RIGHT: Cabinets and seat bases are built from oak, recreating the classy, period look.
BELOW: Twin 240V sockets are located at the base of the television cabinet.

ABOVE: The bulkhead cabinet has been built to contain a television/DVD, with PlayStation console in the base. Note the CD carry-case, finished in matching colours.
BELOW: The L-shaped settee is perfect for sitting and relaxing. Matching scatter cushions add to the look.

Jimi commissioned Vaughn Green and Tim Hartley of Custom Classic and Retro to build the interior to his exact specifications: unlike many owners he had a very clear idea of what he wanted in terms of layout, fittings and colours, and the final design is very close to his original brief. The bus was not to be used for serious camping holidays: it was much more for sitting and 'chilling' in with friends at shows or weekends away. Comfortable seating for a group of friends in an L-shape, sleeping space, and a television/DVD and iPod dock were the basic requirements.

The L-shaped seating comprises a rock-and-roll bed that meets an under-window bench, with a curved corner. The base is built from polished oak, as is the roof cabinet and the television cabinet sited by the load door, retaining that period feel; but the fabrics and uphol-stery reflect very modern materials and

designs. Jimi did not want to introduce new colours into the interior, and it is therefore colour matched to the exteri-or paint, with beige grey vinyl as the base colour for seating and panels. Alcantara, a rich fabric used in *haute couture* and in quality cars such as Mer-cedes, was chosen for contrasting inserts because of its soft suede look and feel, combined with its washable qualities. A new colour range had just been introduced, one of which was a very close match to the deep Titian Red shade; however, it had to be ordered in from Norway.

The centre panels on seats and door cards are trimmed in the soft Alcantara fabric, with a distinctive diamond-stitch pattern design, another of Jimi's requests. He also specified the diagonal-stitching on the corners of each seat base, to break up the smooth surface of the vinyl. Joining areas of fabric and

RIGHT: The rock-and-roll rear seat required some adaptation to fit the interior layout design, and provides an instant bed.

BELOW: The spare wheel is trimmed to match, and the coordinating check curtains are quickly removable and held in place by magnets sewn in the seams.

vinyl on door cards feature grey piping, which is also used on seat and cushion edges. Coordinating single colour scatter cushions add to the look, and Jimi has even made up a matching CD carrycase from some fabric scraps. The spare wheel is also finished in Alcantara and vinyl. The headliner, sunroof and window surrounds are trimmed with soft, light grey velour-style material as used on Jaguar cars, which blends perfectly and adds to the luxurious feel of the interior. Soft burgundy carpet and cab floor mats, with overlocked grey vinyl edges, complete the fully coordinated look. A set of red and white gingham curtains, normally stored to keep the interior lines clean, can be quickly fixed to the windows by means of magnets in the corners and seams.

ABOVE: Attention to detail can be seen in the way the seat back panels have been finished.
BELOW: Cab doors are trimmed to match, and have polished ally grab handles to match exterior brightwork and trim.

BELOW: The stitching detail on the cab seat corners breaks up the smoothness of the vinyl.

ABOVE: The sunroof is just one of the attractive features of a Samba, and light just pours in.
LEFT: The headliner, window surrounds and sunroof base are trimmed in a soft, light grey velour-type fabric.

The television/DVD cabinet was built to fit the monitor Jimi had already sourced, and the lower section has the power invertor and the recent addition of a PlayStation console. Twin 240V sockets are located on its base by the gangway. Storage space is under the rear seat; the long bench seat contains twin amps and 12in sub-woofers; the roof unit has the head unit and two additional storage areas. Speakers are located in the base of the roof locker and cab doors, giving full surround-sound experience. A very neat touch is the iPod docking station built into the dash ashtray.

This is a bus to relax in, elegant and comfortable, and with the sunroof rolled back and light pouring in, what better way to savour the summer? It has taken four years to get the bus looking how Jimi wants it – now he can finally get out and enjoy it.

RIGHT: A novel touch is the siting of an iPod dock in the dash tray.
BELOW: The rock-and-roll seat meets the window seat with a gentle curve, rather than a sharp angle.

angel
2005 T5

ABOVE: *Finger holes make for clean lines on the cabinets. The table can be folded back to become a smaller version, giving more space.*
RIGHT: *The interior is finished in calming blue tones, echoing the watersports theme, and hard-wearing, wipe-clean fabrics and laminates used for practicality.*

This T5 conversion, designated Angel, is the prototype from the Welsh conversion firm Amdro, known well for their alternative camper conversions on the T4 base. Their slogan is 'Making a Difference in the Outdoor World' and they have designed the interior around the key concepts of simplicity, practicality and responsibility, creating an interior that is geared to the outdoor and sports market, and is as environmentally friendly as possible. Thus the cooker is fuelled by methylated spirit, not gas;

lighting is low power LEDs; the fridge is a 12V compressor version that runs off the leisure battery, which in turn is charged from a solar panel on the roof; and natural, sustainable materials have been used throughout. Laminates and fabrics have been specifically chosen for their rugged, hard-wearing qualities, to cope with the outdoor leisure use. The exterior is inspired by the early campers, with bright colours and a splash of chrome. The name 'Angel' has been given to convey that the van will

be delivering a message everywhere it goes, as well as proving to be an angel to all who use it!

The interior layout has been designed as a simple-to-fit DIY kit. All the furniture goes together like a jigsaw, with slots and tabs to locate before screwing into the pre-drilled pilot holes. All the hinges are integrated into the design by clever computer-aided design, and the furniture is easily fitted and equally easily removable to make for a true multi-purpose vehicle.

ABOVE: The rear space is perfect for carrying bikes securely.

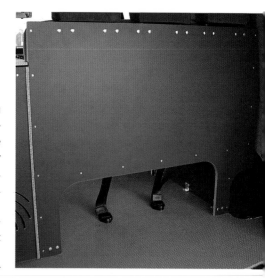

The non-slip commercial ply floor bolts to the existing lashing points on the van, and the furniture all attaches securely to pre-drilled holes in the floor. Sustainable wood has been used throughout, with cabinets made from birch ply, which has been pre-faced with hard-wearing laminate originally developed for playground furniture. Natural materials have been used for heat and sound insulation, with sheep's wool for the sides, and hemp for the roof and floor.

The seat upholstery, roof and side-wall lining is all made from a hard-wearing brushed velour fabric as used by the medical industry, which is stain-proof, waterproof and fire retardant but also washable – the seat covers can be removed and put through a washing machine. The blue tones on seat uphol-stery, cabinets and side panels create tranquillity, and were chosen initially due to the corporate colour scheme, inspired by the outdoors and blue skies.

Instant floor space can be achieved by having the table fold up against the side wall, and the front bench seat hinge up behind the front cab seat, and by removing the front panel – ideal for that fridge you've just bought and need to carry home, or extra bikes for the children. There is an optional stor-age area under the facing bench seat, which features a removable centre panel to create floor space running the full length of the van – perfect for carrying surfboards or skis. The full-

ABOVE: The large open space at the rear is big enough to cope with climbing and camping gear. Note how the rear bulkhead and seat base is open, allowing surfboards to be pushed under and carried inside.

BELOW: The side unit contains a 12V compressor fridge that runs off the leisure battery, and a stainless-steel sink.

The table, finished in blue laminate to match the cabinets, has a hinged extension leaf for dining. Darker blue contrast panels in the seats add relief and styling detail.

width space in the rear behind the seat has also been designed to accommodate two bikes, which means that all your outdoor leisure gear can be safely stored inside the van itself, and can stay there even when the bed is out.

The wide rear seat carries three people and is fitted with head restraints and seat belts. By the side of this is a unit that contains the 12V compressor top-loading fridge and sink, accessed by lift-up tops. At the front of the unit, by the load door, is a small top cupboard with cutlery holder, under which is a larger storage cupboard; the door of this hinges down to form a useful worktop/standing area. Opposite this,

behind the passenger seat, is the cooker unit, with lift-up top and more storage under. The table is used to form the bed base, unfolding down between the bench seat to make a roomy, long bed – something that individuals over 6ft 2in (2m) will appreciate! The table is also hinged, allowing for two different sizes to be used. A surround-sound hi-fi system and DVD player provide entertainment and keep the children happy on those long journeys, with a 9.2in screen mounted on the driver's seat headrest, and extra pop-out 7in screen and control unit in the front. It also has built in iPod control so there is no need to carry hundreds of CDs.

ABOVE: The table can be folded up flat against the side wall, and the front bench hinges up to create a large floor area for instant space.
LEFT: The walls are lined with sheep's wool and trimmed in a lighter blue fabric. Lighting is provided by low-wattage LED strips and touch-control spotlights.

ABOVE: The interior is designed as a simple-to-fit DIY kit; a non-slip commercial ply floor bolts to the lashing points inside the van, and the furniture all attaches securely to pre-drilled holes in the floor. The seatbelts mount through the chassis and to existing wall-mounting positions.

VW themselves recognized the importance of the camping and leisure market by introducing their own factory-fitted camping interior, the California, for the T5 base, something they had never previously done, and the T5 model is growing in popularity very quickly. However, apart from the irritating sliding door on the 'wrong side' on right-hand-drive Californias, they are also quite pricey, and this affordable, easy-to-fit and eco-friendly practical T5 interior offers a different route. Amdro has come up with an interior solution perfectly geared to flexible leisure use that does not need access to full campsite facilities, and is specifically designed to the needs of the outdoor lifestyle. At the time of writing the only interior colour available is blue, but there are plans to offer red and green colour schemes, and Amdro is marketing both DIY kits supported by instructional videos and complete and ready-to-go Angels that are based on recycled and reborn ex-lease vans. **(Additional photographs courtesy of Iwan Lloyd Roberts)**

LEFT: The cooker is an eco-friendly methylated spirit version, located in the top of the unit behind the front passenger seat, with storage cupboard under.

BELOW: The full length, wide double bed, made up by folding down the table, is perfect for taller people.

the boy from Brazil
2005 Brazilian Microbus

LEFT: The seat is easily removable to create more living space when the van is camped up.
BELOW: A single seat, made from the original Microbus bench, is sited by the load door and upholstered to match the cab seats.

For travelling, the seat faces forwards and the cabinet in front of it has a flip-up door that acts as a table.

VW Brazil still produces new transporters based on the Bay window model, and this is one of the last of the air-cooled Bay versions to have been built. It was imported as a Microbus by VW Down Under. Finished in white, the first changes that new owner Gregory Smith made was to convert it to right-hand drive, fit an elevating roof, and have the lower body painted in Turkis for that classic two-tone look (Paul Mullinger of VW Down Under did the paint and the right-hand-drive conversion). Greg wanted a new camper, not an old one requiring endless work, but he also wanted the period styling and look of

the classic VW Campervan, so finding a new Bay window upon which to put his own stamp was the perfect answer.

Having seen the distinctive and individual look of the interiors designed and built by Simon Weitz of Interior Motive, he knew Simon would build a classy, bespoke interior that would combine practicality and contemporary style.

The camper was to be used as a family camper, with two double beds, washing, cooking and storage facilities. The family were well used to tenting, and the interior had to be easy to keep clean, especially on muddy sites.

LEFT: The rear seat is upholstered with a button finish, and a swivel table is mounted at the side. Table and worktops are all finished in Bermuda – a turquoise-blue laminate.

BELOW: Interior panels reverse the upholstery design, with wide stitched turquoise centre sections.

ABOVE: The single seat can face backwards for dining.

BELOW: The cab seats have a stitched pattern with turquoise piping for contrast.

The Turkis exterior has been carried through to the inside, with harmonizing shades of green and blue for work surfaces and table tops, carpet upholstery and interior panels – but it is the striped wood-grain finish to the cabinet work that catches most eyes first. Greg had seen Zebrano wood furniture at an exhibition, and had been immediately drawn to its decorative nature. It is an uncommon hardwood much valued by woodworking artisans; light gold in colour, with narrow streaks of dark brown to almost black, the surface is lustrous.

Greg also liked the curves that Simon creates and works with in his interior designs, so when he saw a Smev hob/sink unit with three burners and curving fronts, he knew the direction in which he wanted the interior to flow. The kitchen cabinet containing the

A Dometic fridge takes up half of the kitchen unit.

A long unit running to the rear under the windows is topped with Bermuda laminate and features three top-accessed storage compartments.

Smev unit is the main unit in the van, with the contours following the double curves. Zebrano veneer has been used to face the cabinet, and no exterior handles interfere with the clean lines. A Dometic fridge is sited on the left with two runs of drawers, three small and three large. Another cabinet runs from this under the windows to the rear, at a slightly lower height than the sink/hob sections, and has three lift-top storage areas. This has been given a work surface of Bermuda laminate, chosen because of its harmonizing blue-green shade, and the Smev unit is inset into a worktop in the same shade. The table top is also finished to match. The front of the long cupboard, the rear bench seat and side cabinet are all finished in Zebrano for design unity.

The rear seat is a rock-and-roll bed, with a swivel table mounted by the sliding door. The single seat was made from the original Microbus bench seat, which Simon cut down and rewelded so that it fitted the space. It faces forwards for travelling, and backwards for dining at the table, and is easily removable when they are camped up, to create more living space. The bulkhead cabinet by the load door in front of this seat has a flip-up door to make a table, and also contains an X Box and controls

ABOVE: Linked television/DVD screens are mounted in the cab roof, on the dash, and on the rear of the driver's headrest.

BELOW: A dash tray, finished in Bermuda with Zebrano-lined open sections, provides handy storage. Note the finishing details such as wooden door pulls, Zebrano trim insets on wiper handles and dashboard, and a wooden gear knob.

ABOVE: Steel-coloured laminate has been used to line bed-board bases, the rear roof section and window pelmets.

in the lower section. Above the cabinet attached to the headrest is a screen hooked to both the X Box and a Freeview television tuner/DVD. Another flip-down screen is mounted in the roof between the cab seats, and there is another smaller pop-up screen in the dash. All three can be linked or can work independently, allowing parents to watch television whilst children can play on the X Box using headphones.

The seats and interior panels have been trimmed by Bernard Newbury using coordinating grey-green and turquoise blue to harmonize. The cab seats and single seat have stitched centre panels, with blue piping detail for the edges and between the stitched and plain sections, whilst the rear seat and bed cushion have been finished with a button effect and blue piping to make a design break. Interior panels reverse the design, with stitched turquoise centre sections.

The flooring is green vinyl that matches the seat upholstery, with loose turquoise-green carpets overlocked with blue edging. Another double bed has been built into the roof, with matching cushions, and pelmets and the undersides of the bed bases and rear roof are finished in steel-coloured laminate. Speakers have been built in under the rear roof panel, and eight touch-operation circular touch lights are mounted on the pelmets and next to the speakers.

The cab features a specially designed, one-off dash tray in matching Bermuda laminate with Zebrano-lined open sections for handy storage; and finishing details such as wooden door pulls, Zebrano trim insets on wiper handles and dashboard, and a wooden gear knob add additional personal touches that tie in the design and colours. Coordinated curtains in matching shades will add the final detailing.

BELOW: Circular touch-operated lights are mounted on the pelmets and roof rear.

For many owners a complete interior refit or redesign is not an option, either because the existing furniture is in sound condition and does not need replacing or updating, or simply because of the expense involved in rebuilding a new interior. Several examples here show how an interior can be modernized and brightened up, and given a striking new look by changing and updating the fabrics. Seats and cushions can be re-covered, and curtains replaced using bright modern designs and materials that completely transform an interior appearance – and new colours and funky patterns can lighten and brighten an interior for a contemporary and individual look.

1980 Devon Moonraker

Richard Newton's 1980 Devon Moonraker has been treated to a styling makeover that has preserved the original cabinets and layout, but by bringing in new colours and materials has updated the look. After the bus had been resprayed in Burgundy Red under Cream, the interior looked a bit past its sell-by date, with brown Dralon upholstery that did not really fit in with the new paint. They decided vinyl would recreate a classic look (as well as being family friendly) and commissioned Tim Avery of Traffic Trim in Wolverhampton to re-cover all the seats and interior panels in matching Burgundy, with cream leather piping on the seats for contrast and to coordinate with the cabinet work and exterior colour scheme. New doors for all cabinets were made up from MDF and sprayed in the same Burgundy as used on the exterior, with new polished aluminium handles. Richard's wife, Ange, made up the curtains using a check plaid period-style fabric from Dunelm. New marble-effect vinyl flooring completes the look.

(Photographs courtesy of Richard Newton)

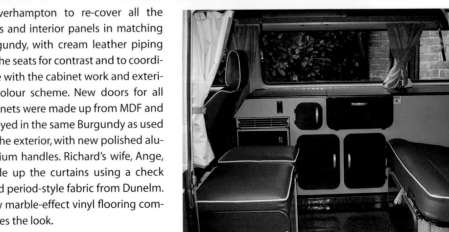

1963 Sundial Camper

Steve Tansey has completely rebuilt from scratch the interior of this 1963 Sundial Camper, and has faithfully recreated the original layout with wood cabinets, interior panels and headlining. American white oak veneer has been used for all interior panelling and cabinets, and the floor tiles have been chosen to match the exterior Turkis (turquoise) colour. The Trimming Tonic reupholstered the seats and cab door panels using a brown vinyl that feels very soft to the touch and blends well with the wood, and the square stitch-pattern centre sections in a lighter brown faux suede make for an individual and distinctive styling detail. Grey-green curtains with subtle stripe sections harmonize the look. Whilst the interior recreates the Sundial look, the bus was never intended to be stock, and adding these individual touches is part of what owning a bus is all about.

1989 Holdsworth Villa 3

Paul Goode's 1989 Holdsworth Villa 3 has been given a modern styling update simply by having the rear and buddy seat reupholstered and by fitting new curtains. The fabric is patterned soft velour from Martrim, and was chosen to reflect the style and colour of the original VW cab seat fabric. Foam wrapped in wadding was used to give an initial soft feel before the firmness of the cushion and the buttoning detail breaks up the slab-like feel of the long cushions. Curtains and matching bolsters were made up by VW Camper Curtains, with the thin stripe design adding contrast and the colours harmonizing with the headlining and blue carpet, showing how new upholstery and curtains can transform an interior.

1973 Devon

This Devon was converted in 1973, and over time has had its interior furniture changed and a Holdsworth pop-top roof added. The new Amulet Red under Ivory Beige paintwork was chosen to coordinate with a red/cream check material that owner Jo Farrington had already sourced from IKEA in order to revamp the interior herself. The main cushions have a button finish with piped edges, and matching bolsters are customized with a cream VW logo. The red and cream striped Alvine Smal curtains were made from pre-packed curtain panels, with covered buttons that match the seat buttoning for the tiebacks. Spare curtain material has been used to make deckchair covers and a quilt bag. The coordinating red heart and hands cushion also came from IKEA and adds a funky touch. Red fleece blankets from Woolworths have been turned into quilts and a hot water bottle cover, all with embroidered VW logos.

The cab seats were professionally done by Parkers of Douglas, Isle of Man, using Lionella vinyl in Rich Red and Oatmeal with stitched centre panels and piping. Everything else in the interior has been done by Jo herself, including using the same colour vinyls to re-cover the door panels, buddy seat base and front panel of the rock-and-roll bed, and adding contrasting stitching. Over time Jo has sourced and added a variety of colour-coordinated accessories including a cream and red striped rug, a red spot enamelled bucket and mini milk churn, red towels, red kettle, red spot cutlery, cream and red tea towels with a butterfly motif, and a red spot toast rack and mugs. Jo says every time she goes into a shop she sees something to add! The interior has a warm, cheerful, lived-in look, and as the bus is used for camping all the time with a dog, the removable washable covers and wipe-clean vinyl are practical as well as stylish. With a red-themed interior and bright red paint there could only be one name for this lovely camper: Poppy.

(Photographs courtesy of Jo Farrington)

1967 SO 42

Martin Hall, of Martin Hall Imports in Southampton, is responsible for a complete bare metal restoration on this 1967 Westfalia SO 42 camper, now owned by Phil Taylor. Just about everything you can imagine has been done, including a repaint in the original Pearl White by Martin Harper. The interior has also been fully refurbished, with cabinets repaired and revarnished, and the spice rack cabinet was remade from scratch using wood from scrapped Westfalia parts. All the birch side panels and headliner have also been replaced to recreate the original period look. Subtle pastels were chosen for the upholstery and curtains to tone with the natural wood interior and white paintwork, making for a contemporary look. Rather than recreate the dated feel of the original goldy brown, cream vinyl has been used to reupholster the seats to provide light, and the neutral shade complements the warm wood tones perfectly. The front seats have been stitch pleated to make a design break with the smooth rear seat cushions. The fabric for the curtains was supplied by VW Curtains, and they are striped in pastel greys and blue, providing an understated touch of colour whilst harmonizing with the exterior. The stock look to the interior has been maintained, but new fabrics and colours add a modern feel that is fully in keeping with period styling. *(Photographs courtesy of Phil Taylor)*

1960 Microbus

Mark Boardman has gone for the minimalist look with his right-hand-drive camper, and has created a bright, easy-to-maintain look with plenty of space. Apart from a KW Conversions rock-and-roll bed, the solid oak floor of the whole load area is clear. The polished metal bed frame is left open, revealing the chromed heater outlet and lower bulkhead and wheel arches, which are covered with wood panel and oatmeal carpet. The headlining is panelled in matching wood ply, with polished aluminium pelmet panels above the windows, and aluminium roof and air vent trim that reflect and enhance natural light. The interior panels are trimmed in oatmeal vinyl, with piped dividing to edge the oatmeal carpet centre panels, and have been fixed using industrial strength Velcro to maintain the clean look with no fittings showing. The rear

bench has been upholstered in matching vinyl, with a stitched pattern, whilst the front bench seat has vertical pleats. The large open space is designed so that all the camping gear can be boxed and easily carried when travelling, and with the sunroof open the interior feels incredibly spacious. Finishing details include Deluxe coathooks and chrome bling in the cab including pedals, handbrake, gear stick and door tops.

(Photographs courtesy of Tom Steele)

1973 Westfalia Camper

The Westfalia Camper shown here was built in 1973 and features all the original period cabinets and fittings. Owner Stef Leonard had it resprayed in original orange/white colours, and the inside has been retrimmed to give an updated look to the interior. The seats and panels have been reupholstered in grey with orange piping detail by Chris at Trimming Tonic in Nelson, Lancashire, and Sarah at VW Camper Cushions made up the curtains and cushions in an orange and white hibiscus garland pattern fabric to bring coordinating colour with a hint at the surfing tradition. The addition of a red and white hibiscus flower floormat, from Flowers Up, echoes the surfing and flower theme, and the new upholstery and curtains modernize and brighten the stock interior.

(Photographs courtesy of Stef Leonard)

1990 Autohomes Komet

This 1990 2.1 petrol injection T3, owned by Brendan O'Farrell, was converted as an Autohomes Komet from new. The interior needed no refurbishment, but the dated beige upholstery has been given a fresh look by having all the seats re-covered in Stuart Tartan from Fabricaz (www.fabricaz.co.uk) by Paul Duffy of Stageone in Coventry. Break out the whisky!

(Photographs courtesy of Brendan O'Farrell)

1979 Panel Van

Designed and built by owner Kieron Marshall, this interior has been built using beech wood laminate flooring packs and veneered ply panels to make up the cabinets with polished steel handles and catches to add to the contemporary look. Cooker, sink, top-

accessed coolbox and ample storage are in the run under the side windows, with the walk-through and seat bulkhead also panelled around. In the rear are more cupboards running to the roof. What is probably most striking, however, is the use of bold leopard-skin prints, in harmonizing colours with the beechwood, to cover seats and interior panels, finished off with a matching rug over the beech flooring. Coordinating detail is provided by tiger-skin print fabrics for the curtains, including a door curtain hanging by the sliding door for fresh air, shade and privacy. The resulting interior is a bright, light, modern look that hints at exotic safari and adventure.

1983 Panel Van

Peter Boxall has given this 1983 panel van a whole new look, inspired by the Euro Look T3 Project Bus and the Porsche styling, with distinctive Aegean Blue metallic paint (from the Peugeot range), blue LEDs and neons in the interior, Porsche alloys, steering wheel and glovebox lock, rev counter and Big Foot gas pedal. The rear seat/rock-and-roll bed (the frame of which was from a Bay found outside a workshop) is trimmed in light grey, as are the cab seats. Royal blue contrast detailing has been added to the cab seats, and the interior panels are fin-ished in mottled grey unribbed auto carpet with royal blue centre sections. The roof lining was a kit made by AVA Leisure and oak laminate flooring in grey shades has been fitted to harmonize with the interior greys. The whole floor has been kept clear, giving a sense of open space, and a flip-down LCD TV/DVD is mounted in the cab for entertainment. At night the neon blue lights make for a stunning effect that really sets off the paint and colour scheme. Peter did all the interior work himself, and is now ready for the next project!

(Photographs courtesy of Pete Boxall)

Flowers for Colour

Imitation flowers and flower garlands are excellent ways of bringing colour and warmth into an interior, and come in many varieties and shades. Colour-coordinated gerberas or sprays of edelweiss are ideal for bud vases, whilst garlands of hibiscus hanging from the mirror bring in that Hawaiian surf touch. Flowers always brighten, cheer and dress our homes, and a bus interior is the same. Companies such as Flowers Up, bus enthusiasts themselves, offer a vast range of colours and flowers, of which just a few are shown here, as well as a range of fun accessories such as hula girls and monkeys.

(Photographs courtesy of David Bunce)

gazetteer

The following list is the contact details for individuals and companies whose work and products are featured in this book. Many have websites with full galleries showcasing their work, which are well worth visiting.

Anderson Ryan
Coventry
02476 712222
www.andersonryan.com

Amdro Alternative Camper Conversions
Iwan Lloyd Roberts
Caernarfon
Gwynedd LL55 4EZ
08704 322032
www.amdro.co.uk
ian@amdro.co.uk

Bernard Newbury Auto Interiors
1 Station Road
Leigh-on-Sea
Essex
SS9 1ST
01702 710211
www.bernardnewbury.co.uk

Bluebird Customs
Great Harwood
Lancs
01254 888416
www.bluebird-type2.co.uk

Calypso Campers
Jon Freemantle
The Lower Barn
Chilhampton Farm
Wilton
Salisbury
Wiltshire SP2 0AB
01722 744777
www.calypsocampers.co.uk

Custom Classic and Retro Auto Interiors
Loughborough
Leics.
Vaughn Green
07950 331759
01509 558616
Tim Hartley
0794 6304497
01509 210736
www.customclassicretro.co.uk

Custom Made Furniture Ltd
Neil Roberts
Unit 16d
Chalwyn Industrial Estate
Poole
Dorset
BH12 4PE
01202 737555

DB Cartrim
Blackpool
Lancashire
01253 894999
07786 575728
dbrigden@btinternet.com
www.dbcartrim.com

Evans Trim
199 Peterborough Road,
Whittlesey
Peterborough
Cambridgeshire
PE7 1PD
01733 205980
www.evans-trim.co.uk

Flowers-Up!
Springside
Bells Walk
Wrington
North Somerset
BS40 5PU
01934 862603
www.flowers-up.com

Interior Motive
Simon Weitz
07830 183190
www.interiormotiveuk.com

J & S Upholstery
Unit 42 Askern Ind Est.
Moss Road
Askern
Doncaster
S. Yorkshire
DN6 0DD
01302 709926
Steve@thetrimshack.fsnet.co.uk

Kustom Interiors
The Workshops
Sandylands Farm
Egloshayle
Wadebridge
North Cornwall
PL27 6EL
07910 838 649
www.kustominteriors.co.uk
daron@kustominteriors.co.uk

**Martin Hall Imports
Volkswagen Splitscreen Westfalia Specialist**
Southampton
Hampshire
07775 736488
hallie92@gmail.com
www.hallie.freeserve.co.uk

Martrim
Sandbach
Cheshire
www.martrim.co.uk

MGR Custom Interiors
Matt Gregory
07738 128733
mattygreg05@aol.com
Enquiries@MGR-CustomInteriors.co.uk
www.mgr-custominteriors.co.uk

Pooch
www.pointblankpixels.com

Renzo Rapaccioli
Uley
Gloucestershire
07792 179887

S.J. Bowles
Unit 6B
St Michael's Trading Estate
Bridport
Dorset
DT6 3RR
01308 420091
info@sjbowles.co.uk
www.sjbowles.co.uk

Smev
www.smev.com

Spirit of the Fifties
Sutton Coldfield
01675 479775
www.spiritofthe50s.co.uk

Stage One Upholstery
Paul Duffy
287 Walsgrave Road
Stoke, Coventry
CV2 4BE
02476 636262
www.stageoneupholstery.co.uk

Timber Technicians
Nottingham
0115 9653399
www.timbertechnicians.co.uk

Traffic Trim
Tim Avery
Wolverhampton
07795 183375
traffictrim@aol.com

Trimming Tonic
Chris Lyons
Unit 13
Barnfield Business Centre
Brunswick Street
Nelson
Lancashire
BB9 0HT
01282 605112
07795 243488
chris@trimmingtonic.co.uk
www.trimmingtonic.co.uk

Truwood Furniture Ltd
Bromfield Industrial Estate
Mold
Flintshire
CH7 1JR
01352 750777
www.truwoodfurniture.co.uk

UTS Upholstery
C. Andrews
Buckley
Flintshire
CH7 3HB
01244 546001

Vantasia
Paul and Diane
Unit 10/15
Ridgeway farm
Powick
Worcs
WR2 4SN
01905 831558
07774 716554

VW Camper Curtains Ltd
Sarah Braddon
Three Horse Shoes
Marsh Road
Holbeach Hurn
Lincolnshire
PE12 8JY
01406 422498
07761 568536
www.vwcampercurtains.co.uk

VW Curtains
Andrew Fowler
1 Kensington Road
Sandiacre
Nottingham
NG10 5PD
0701 7436601
www.vwcurtains.com